Irish
MURDERS

Lily Seafield

WAVERLEY BOOKS

Published 2015 by Waverley Books, an imprint of
The Gresham Publishing Company Ltd, Academy Park, Building 4000,
Gower Street, Glasgow, G51 1PR, Scotland

First published 2002. Reprinted 2006, 2008, 2010, 2015.

ISBN 978 1 84934 338 1

Printed and bound in Spain by Novoprint, S.A.

Contents

THE COLLEEN BAWN

In the small graveyard at Burrane, County Clare, lies the body of Ireland's most famous murder victim, Ellie (or Ellen) Hanley. Most Irish people might not recognize the name, but if you were to mention the 'Colleen Bawn', an Irish phrase that translates as the White Girl, they would immediately know whom you were talking about. Her tragic death went down in folk legend, and spawned a succession of nineteenth-century literary works, including novels (Gerald Griffin's The Collegians and Thomas Carleton's Willie Reilly and his Dear Colleen Bawn) a play (Dion Boucicault's The Colleen Bawn) and an opera (Julius Benedict's The Lily of Killarney). After the Irish Potato Famine, emigrants took her story of betrayal and drowning to America, where its echoes are found in traditional ballads such as 'The Knoxville Girl', with its refrain:

Go down, go down you Knoxville girl, with the dark and rolling tide;
Go down, go down you Knoxville girl, you'll never be my bride.'

The fifteen-year-old whose cruel murder encouraged all of these literary outpourings was a simple Irish peasant girl, extremely pretty but without any education or social graces. Ellie Hanley lived with her uncle in a small cottage near Ballycahane in north Limerick. Whilst not quite an orphan, she had been abandoned at a very young age, when her father re-married after the death of her mother. Her mother's brother brought the unwanted child to live with him, and raised her as his adopted daughter. He conscientiously began saving money for a dowry, and by Ellie's fifteenth birthday in 1819 had amassed over a hundred pounds, a large sum for a man in his humble circumstances.

In the early summer of that year, Ellie Hanley attracted the attention of John Scanlan, the heir of Ballycahane Castle. Good looking and still only in his early twenties, he was the scion of an aristocratic family, but had a bad name in the locality due to his dissolute habits. Scanlan, back in Limerick after being cashiered from the Royal Marines, was usually to be found carousing or hunting with his manservant, Stephen Sullivan. The innocent Ellie seems to have been swept off her feet by the handsome ex-officer's courtship. At the beginning of July, a few weeks after their first meeting, the couple eloped without warning, taking the dowry with them.

Scanlan brought Ellie to the village of Glin, on the Limerick bank of the River Shannon. During the following month, she was in the company of another local girl named Ellen Walshe, who briefly acted as her maidservant. Ellie Hanley announced she was now married to John Scanlan, and proudly showed off her trousseau. Later it was discovered that Scanlan had neglected to inform his sister or anybody else of the wedding, which was not genuine but performed by a fake clergyman. It soon became apparent that Scanlan was already bored with the girl, and had begun mistreating her. Ellen Walshe noticed how drawn and haggard she was looking, and was not surprised when her mistress vanished from sight a little while later. Scanlan was unconcerned at the loss of his

young lover, and casually mentioned that she had gone off with a sea captain.

Ellie Hanley's friends asked many questions after her sudden disappearance. Scanlan and Sullivan ignored the bad feeling towards them, and continued to pursue their dissipated lifestyle without interference. Ellen Walshe noticed that they were wearing rings on their little fingers, which resembled those owned by the missing girl. She also saw Sullivan's sister with a fine woollen cloak, which she knew belonged to Ellie Hanley, increasing her suspicions that something terrible had happened to the missing girl. Yet without a body or any evidence of foul play there was little the police of the time could do.

Summer passed, and it was late September when two fishermen made a gruesome discovery on the opposite shore of the Shannon estuary. Washed up on the strand lay the badly decayed body of a young girl, with a rope loosely tied around her body. One arm was completely missing, presumably torn off by some large sea animal, whilst the other had been broken. The fishermen, suspecting that the body was not the result of an accidental drowning, rushed off to report their find at the nearest police barracks in Kilrush, County Clare. The news reached Major Warburton of the Irish Constabulary who was aware of the mysterious disappearance of a girl in Limerick. He immediately informed the magistrate at Glin, who dispatched a representative to examine and hopefully identify the body as Ellie Hanley's. Ellen Walshe and a man named Jack King, a Limerick rope maker, accompanied him. King had lent Scanlan a rope some months previously and never got it back.

The body on the strand, which had been loosely buried in sand to preserve its dignity, was exhumed and the fragile remains examined by the witnesses. Jack King recognized the rope and confirmed it was identical to the one borrowed by Scanlan. Ellen Walshe experienced more difficulty in deciding whether or not the drowned woman was Ellie Hanley. She thought she recognized the torn stays around its midriff as the ones she had tied on her erstwhile mistress, but the face was so rotted that it was impossible to identify. The magistrate asked her if Ellie Hanley had any identifying marks, and the maidservant remembered that the girl had two doubled teeth. They checked the corpse's mouth but all of its teeth had been knocked out, a sinister indication of a violent assault in itself. A doctor was summoned and confirmed that the sockets of the teeth in the jawbone matched Ellen Walshe's description. The girl then agreed that the body was Ellie Hanley's.

Warrants were issued for the arrest of Scanlan and Sullivan, but the Limerick police made no effort to apprehend the wanted men. Scanlan's family was rich and influential, and the authorities feared offending them. In early November, Thomas Spring Rice, the local magistrate, finally lost patience at the delay, and mounted his own surprise raid on Ballycahane Castle with a squad of army lancers. After searching for several hours without finding either suspect, he was about to give up the hunt when Scanlan was found hiding in a haystack. The prisoner, who had been wounded during his arrest, was taken to Limerick Gaol, whilst the hunt for his missing servant continued.

The authorities did not accept Scanlan's story that Ellie Hanley had run off to sea, and he was committed to trial in March 1820. His wealthy family engaged Daniel O'Connell, the most successful Irish barrister of his day, to defend him in court. The lawyer was soon to embark on a political career, which would make him a national hero for leading the struggle for Catholic emancipation and almost gaining Irish independence. O'Connell placed all the blame for Ellie Hanley's death on the vanished Sullivan, a difficult argument to counter since there was no firm evidence to say exactly how she met her fate. The closeness of the two men, however, argued against this. It was unlikely that Sullivan murdered Ellie Hanley without the involvement of his master, who was after all the one with a motive for getting rid of her. The jury declared Scanlan to be guilty of murder, and he was condemned to death.

Scanlan responded to his conviction with an impassioned declaration of his innocence, again swearing that Sullivan had committed the murder without his knowledge. The apparent sincerity of the speech provoked some unease about his guilt. Despite his mother's frantic efforts to gain a last minute reprieve Scanlan went to the gallows on 16 March 1820. The execution turned out to be even more dramatic than his trial. As Scanlan approached the hanging place, the horses drawing his wagon stopped dead and refused to move. Perhaps Scanlan's mother had bribed the driver, since several spectators at once yelled out that this proved the prisoner's innocence.

Scanlan stood up and offered to walk to the gallows cart, which he then proceeded to do. The hood was placed around his head, and the executioner was on the point of signalling for the hanging to begin, when the Sheriff of Limerick intervened. He lifted the hood and asked Scanlan if he wished to confess to the murder of Ellie Hanley before dying. If he hoped Scanlan would silence any doubts about his guilt, the Sheriff was disappointed. The condemned man, after quietly saying he hadn't expected to see the light of day again, once again passionately protested his innocence. The execution proceeded and Scanlan was hanged, but many in the crowd felt they had witnessed a miscarriage of justice.

Had Stephen Sullivan never been apprehended, John Scanlan's declaration of his innocence might today be used to justify a claim that he was wrongly convicted. But if there is one thing the Colleen Bawn murder confirms, it is that lies drop from a murderer's mouth as easily as leaves fall from a chestnut tree in autumn. Scanlan's hapless servant had fled to the neighboring county of Kerry, changed his name to Clinton, and married a local woman. But, running short of funds, he committed a petty fraud and was taken into custody. A fellow prisoner informed on him for the reward on his head, and Sullivan was returned to Limerick to answer for his part in the death of Ellie Hanley.

The trial of the brutish Sullivan was low-key compared to the high drama accompanying that of his elegant master. He could not afford the services of a lawyer, and was so resigned to his fate that he made little effort to defend himself. At his perfunctory trial, the jury declared the servant guilty after a deliberation of only fifteen minutes, following which he inevitably received the death sentence. Before his hanging, the illiterate Sullivan dictated his confession. He fully implicated Scanlan as the instigator and guiding force that directed the murder of Ellie Hanley, whilst admitting he was the one who killed her and disposed of the body.

Scanlan, according to his servant, tired of the girl soon after taking her dowry. Ellie had become a nuisance, and he began pressuring his servant to dispose of her. Sullivan was reluctant at first, but eventually bowed to Scanlan's orders and procured a boat. Their plan was to get Ellie so drunk she passed out, after which Sullivan would row her out into the estuary of the River Shannon. There he would shoot her, tie the body with chains so it could not float to the surface, and throw it into the deep waters of the river. Sullivan's first attempt to carry out the plot failed, since he could not bring himself to pull the trigger on the defenceless child. When he returned to shore, Scanlan was furious to see Ellie still in the boat. He nagged at Sullivan and coerced him into going out again. At his second attempt, Sullivan managed to fire the gun, but botched his shot and hit his target in the arm rather than the head as he intended. Ellie woke from her alcoholic torpor and began screaming, at which Sullivan beat her to death with the butt of his musket. This explained the loss of all her teeth. It was not easy to kill the struggling girl in the small, rocking boat, and during Ellie's death struggles the iron chain fell overboard. Sullivan improvised, and used the boat rope to attach weights to his victim's body before consigning it to the tide. When he came back alone to Glin, his master's only response to Ellie Hanley's murder was a curt 'All right.'

To some extent Sullivan's confession sought to minimize his role in the brutal crime, hoping it might improve his slim hopes of obtaining a pardon. Nonetheless there can be little doubt that Scanlan was the one with the overriding motive for killing his young 'wife'. He had planned and carried out the mock marriage to get his hands on her dowry. This constituted fraud, as well as ruining his chances of making a good marriage later. His family and peers might turn a blind eye to the seduction and deception of a peasant girl – hardly an unusual event in nineteenth-century Ireland but they would not so easily forgive him for fraudulently robbing her uncle, which would irreparably damage his reputation. Once Scanlan obtained her dowry it was inevitable that the unsophisticated Ellie would sooner or later become a burden. How else could he permanently remove himself from this unsuitable union, and hide his fraud, except through murder?

Later literary versions of the Colleen Bawn murder depicted Ellie Hanley and Scanlan as a latter day Romeo and Juliet, who are destroyed by the machinations of the evil Sullivan. In reality, the Limerick aristocrat murdered his gullible lover by proxy, and his ignorant servant was the dupe who put the order into effect. Behind John Scanlan's Byronic good looks and protestations of innocence, there lurked the heart of a cold-blooded killer.

THE IRELAND'S EYE
MYSTERY

If there was one thing our Victorian ancestors liked to read in their morning newspapers it was a good scandal – for preference one involving murder, sex and a sinister but handsome villain. The mysterious drowning of Maria Louisa Kirwan in September 1852 provided these ingredients and more. Her death on a small island off the Irish coast resulted in the controversial murder trial of her husband, which was marred by unsubstantiated rumour and prejudice.

Anybody who has ever sailed into the wide reaches of Dublin Bay will know Ireland's Eye, the rocky island that hangs like a teardrop a few thousand yards off the bulk of Howth Head. In the nineteenth century, a visit to its grassy heights was one of the attractions of the small resort of Howth, a popular haven for wealthier Dubliners during the summer months.

On 6 September 1852, William Bourke Kirwan and his wife Maria, who had been spending the summer in the village, went off on a day trip to the islet; they took a picnic and a bag containing Maria's swimming costume and an easel and paints for William. At about 4 p.m., they were noticed by another couple, who were returning to the mainland after being picked up by William and Patrick Nangle, the local boatmen. Kirwan was sketching, whilst his wife was walking up and down reading. Maria exchanged a few words with the Nangles and told them to return around 8 p.m. It was the last time anybody but her husband saw her alive.

There was nothing about the Kirwans' demeanour on that afternoon which might have predicted the events that were to follow. They might have been any normal middle-class couple enjoying a pleasant day beside the sea. William Bourke Kirwan, a professional artist who specialized in miniature portraits, was in his early thirties in 1852. He came from a wealthy Dublin family with good contacts in the higher circles of society. He was a Protestant, but had chosen to marry a Catholic wife, quite a rare occurrence at that time. They had been married for thirteen years and seemed to be happy enough, although the union had remained childless. Maria Kirwan, a strikingly beautiful woman, was several years younger than her husband, whom she met whilst he was teaching pupils to draw at the school owned by her parents. She bathed regularly in the waters off Howth, and was an exceptionally strong swimmer.

The Kirwans were alone on Ireland's Eye for nearly four hours before the boat returned at 7.45 p.m. William Kirwan was standing alone by the jetty. He told the Nangles his wife had gone to swim in the Long Hole, a deep inlet about 120 yards long, and had not returned. At his request, they lit lanterns and began searching the small island. Over an hour later Patrick Nangle saw something white at the entrance of the Long Hole. Clambering down they found the body of Maria Kirwan, lying on a small rock in the sea. She was covered in seaweed, and her long hair flowed out into the receding tide, which had previously hidden her body. Mrs Kirwan was still wearing her swimming costume and boots; a few weeks later her missing swimming cap would be found in the cove.

Kirwan knelt beside his wife, and asked Patrick Nangle to look around for her clothes so he could cover the body. When the boatman came back empty handed, the husband went off to find them. Nangle was surprised to see him come back with the items a few minutes later, from a direction where the man later claimed he had already searched. The disputed incident that now followed contributed to the later allegation that Maria Kirwan was murdered. According to Kirwan, the bundle of clothes included his wife's bath sheet, which he wrapped around her. Patrick Nangle disagreed: he said the body had already been lying on the sheet when they found it. The position of the bath sheet was to become a key element in the case against William Kirwan.

It was now evening. The Nangles departed to get their boat, so they could bring it round to Long Hole. They left the weeping husband holding his wife in his arms. After picking up the dead woman, the boatmen returned to Howth, where a crowd was waiting on the pier. The body was removed to the parlour of Margaret Campbell, the Kirwans' landlady, to be laid out for burial. There was already talk that the woman had been murdered, and Father Hall, the local parish priest, warned a police constable to keep an eye on her husband. Kirwan insisted that the body of his wife be washed immediately, and three Howth women undertook the harrowing task. They found a number of scratches on the body, which they attributed to the activities of sea crabs, and large quantities of blood pouring from its ears. The local coroner was aware of the vehement accusations that were circulating around the community. He ordered the body to be examined by a doctor, and arranged an inquest for the following day.

The inquest cleared Kirwan of any malicious involvement

in the tragedy. James Hamilton, a sixth-year medical student who examined the body, stated that Maria Kirwan had drowned accidentally. The only discordant note was the issue of the bath sheet. Yet when Patrick Nangle suggested that Maria Kirwan had been lying on it when they discovered the body, both his brother and the dead woman's husband contradicted him. The boatman was forced to admit he might have made a mistake, and Kirwan left the coroner's court with his reputation unstained. This should have ended the outcry against the artist, but in fact his troubles were only beginning. The next day, as Kirwan left Howth to bring his wife's body to Dublin, the Nangles came up and began abusing him. They claimed he owed them money, and shouted he had got away with murdering his wife. Kirwan eventually calmed them down and drove off, but it was an omen of the tide of innuendo and public hysteria by which he would shortly be engulfed.

Not long after the funeral, a woman named Maria Byrne made some startling allegations. Mrs Byrne, a widow, seems to have had a long-term grudge against Kirwan, and had already accused him of a number of other crimes, including trying to poison Maria Kirwan. The claims had been investigated by the police and found to be groundless. According to Mrs Byrne, the apparently model husband had a secret mistress and eight children. The truth of this statement was confirmed when a woman named Teresa Kenny and her children moved in with the 'grieving' widower within weeks of his wife's death. The relationship had predated Kirwan's involvement with his legal wife by several years. Kirwan had divided his time up equally between the two women, spending a half of the week with each. Such a peculiar arrangement was by no means unique. At least one of the artist's contemporaries, the noted surgeon Sir William Wilde (father of Oscar Wilde), maintained a second family. Others were no doubt discreetly doing the same, but in Kirwan's case the scandal fuelled more rumours about the death of his legal wife.

As feeling against the widower mounted, unsubstantiated reports began to appear in the Dublin newspapers. Kirwan was reported to have regularly beaten Maria, and articles were published attributing several other murders to him. One month after the drowning, the authorities responded to the demands of the press and public for action in the case. They exhumed the victim's body from the damp earth of Dublin's only Catholic cemetery at Glasnevin, and sent it to a pathologist, Dr George Hatchell, for examination. Despite its poor condition, Hatchell quickly reached a decision as to the cause of death. Maria, he reported, had not been drowned, but smothered or asphyxiated. Kirwan was immediately arrested by the police and charged with her murder.

The trial of William Bourke Kirwan commenced on 8 December 1852. The accused man chose Sir Isaac Butt to represent him in court. Butt is still considered to have been one of the great Irish barristers. He was also a leading political figure of the era, and the founder of the Irish Home Rule Party. The dice were loaded against the prisoner from the beginning, since the early Victorian legal system was heavily tilted in favour of the prosecution. At that time, there was no Book of Evidence to help lawyers prepare a defence in advance of a trial. Barristers had to defend their clients without prior knowledge of what witnesses might be called to testify. There was no Appeal Court to approach after a verdict was handed down, and an accused man was not allowed to testify in his own defence. This last rule was particularly crippling for Kirwan's defence, since his personal denials of guilt might have swayed the jury in his favour.

The prosecution alleged that Kirwan's wife had found out about his mistress some six months previously. She was shocked, and demanded he renounce Teresa and her brood of children. Kirwan was not willing to do this, and was tired of his lawful wife. He decided the only way out of his impasse was to remove her from the scene. When the opportunity arose on Ireland's Eye he smothered Maria with her own bath sheet and threw her into the sea to simulate a drowning accident. Several witnesses related that they were on Howth Head that evening, and heard screams coming from the island around 7 p.m. It was presumed these were the screams of Maria Kirwan as she struggled with her murderous husband. The women who washed the body of the victim testified that the cuts and bruises were too serious to be a result of an accident. The victim was covered in blood, and they had not seen similar damage on other drowned bodies they laid out.

Margaret Campbell, the Kirwan's landlady, told the Court of a fierce argument in which Maria Kirwan had been brutally beaten by her husband; she had heard him threaten to kill her. She added that Kirwan's trousers were soaking wet when he got back to the boarding house from the island, even though he had not been in the sea. Patrick Nangle was a key prosecution witness against Kirwan. He took the stand to relate his story about the missing clothes and the bath sheet, embellishing the account with a new detail. He swore Kirwan was carrying a swordstick, and recalled noticing a deep stab wound in Maria's Kirwan's chest. Finally Dr

Hatchell testified that Maria Kirwan had been smothered, although Butt forced him to admit he could not entirely rule out the possibility of drowning.

The evidence of some of these witnesses, compared to their answers at the Howth inquest, was extremely hostile. Even though Butt mounted a spirited defence, he was hampered by the damage already caused to his client's reputation by gossip and the accusations of the press. Nevertheless he succeeded in denting the case against Kirwan. Patrick Nangle was revealed under cross-examination to be biased and unreliable, and Butt argued that the position of the bath sheet was irrelevant anyway. A drowning woman struggling to get back on shore might well have grabbed at it and been entangled. Lastly, the barrister demolished Dr Hatchell's theories about the cause of death. He explained that Maria Kirwan had been prone to a form of epilepsy, and had previously taken several fits on dry land. If one of these had come on her whilst swimming, Mrs Kirwan could easily have suffocated in the manner described by the doctor.

The jury deliberated for over four hours before reaching a guilty verdict. Kirwan, on receiving the mandatory death sentence, declared he did not murder Maria: 'I had no hand, act or part in, or knowledge of my late wife's death.' He was then led off to await execution.

By no means everybody who followed the trial believed that the verdict was correct. Alexander Boyd, who had been the foreman of the Howth inquest jury, ran three days of acoustic tests to demonstrate that screams from Ireland's Eye could not be heard from Howth. Maria Kirwan's mother came forward to give her son-in-law a glowing character reference, whilst Teresa Kenny confirmed she and Maria Kirwan had known about each other for years, although they had not actually met until six months previously.

The most telling argument against the conviction of Kirwan appeared in an article by Dr Arthur Swaine Taylor. The great English scientist, who was one of the founders of forensic pathology, concluded that 'Death was not the result of homicidal drowning or suffocation, but most probably from a fit resulting from natural causes.' This opinion was publicly agreed with by many of Dublin's leading doctors and surgeons. The growing weight of evidence suggesting Kirwan was innocent left the authorities in a quandary. The only person who could quash the verdict was the Lord Lieutenant, the Crown's representative in Ireland. If he pardoned the artist, he would appear to be criticizing the Irish judiciary. Rather than take this drastic action he commuted the sentence to life imprisonment.

William Bourke Kirwan had escaped the gallows, but he would be an old man before he regained his freedom. After a short spell in Spike Island, the prison fortress in Cork harbour, he was transported to the English prison colony on Bermuda. He served eight years on the island, until his health began to fail. Kirwan was returned to Spike Island, where he spent another sixteen years in captivity before finally being released in 1879, on the condition he leave the British Isles. He sailed to New York to be reunited with Teresa Kenny and her family, who had settled in the slums of Brooklyn after being driven out of Ireland by poverty. He is believed to have died shortly afterwards, worn out by his twenty-six years of incarceration for a murder that most likely never occurred.

THE DERRYVEAGH MURDER

On 13 November 1860, James Murray, the Scottish steward
of the Derryveagh Estate in County Donegal, went out to
look for some lost sheep. He did not come home that evening, and two days passed before a search party found his
body in the hills above the Glenveagh valley. His head had
been battered in with a large stone, and in his hand was his
revolver, from which one shot had been discharged. John
George Adair, the unpopular owner of the estate, believed
the crime was committed by his tenants, and instigated one
of the most notorious mass evictions in Irish history. Yet
nobody was convicted for the crime, and the police could
not produce any evidence to implicate the Irish peasants
of Derryveagh in it. Who killed James Murray remains
an unanswered question, but there are strong reasons
for believing that the murder had nothing to do with the
Derryveagh tenants.

The murder took place against a background of land
agitation in Donegal and the other western counties of
Ireland that had been provoked by the activities of greedy
land speculators. The unrest was caused by their policy of
evicting tenants and replacing them with commercial sheep
farming. The peasants, whose homes and livelihoods were
threatened, struck back by maiming the landlords' Scottish
sheep, and sometimes by assaulting or assassinating their
agents and employees. Between 1857 and 1878 more than

21

one hundred murders were committed over land disputes, a large number of which took place in Donegal. These included the most notorious of all Irish 'land-war' atrocities – the murder of the hated Lord Leitrim and two of his employees in 1878.

It was probably inevitable that George Adair's ruthless farming practices would lead to bloodshed and tragedy in Derryveagh. From the moment he bought the estate, there was bad feeling between him and the tenants, who had rented their lands for generations from the previous owners. One bone of contention was Adair's confiscation of common land, aimed at preventing the rams of Irish farmers from impregnating his expensive imported sheep. Another was the behaviour of his roughneck Scottish shepherds, a hard-drinking group of men with a reputation for dishonesty and depravity. Part of their job was to intimidate the Irish tenants, and at least two of them were later gaoled for assaults and shootings. Tensions between the local people and Adair's thuggish employees, already high, rose steeply after he issued a year's notice of eviction to his tenants in November 1859. This had recently come into effect when James Murray's murder took place.

The Royal Irish Constabulary, who investigated the crime, at first concentrated on a member of one of the numerous Sweeney families in the valley, and a tenant called Manus Rodden. The Sweeneys had recently quarrelled with James Murray, whilst Rodden had been working on the mountainside at the time of the steward's murder. He was cutting hazel rods for thatching, a pile of which lay close to the body. Apart from this circumstantial evidence, there was nothing else to connect these suspects with the murder, and they were soon released without being charged. The police appeared to be unable to solve the crime, since no local people were prepared to help them track down the murderer. Then a man named William Deery, who was prepared to inform on the killers of Murray for the substantial reward that had been offered, contacted them.

Deery claimed to be a member of the Ribbonmen, an agrarian secret society which was thought to be active in Donegal. The informer named several members of the shadowy terrorist group as the perpetrators of previous attempted murders and assaults. He stated he had witnessed the murder of James Murray by a mob of one hundred and twenty tenants. Murray, he said, was able to fire only one shot from his pistol before being overwhelmed; this hit and badly wounded a man named Bradley. The police eagerly accepted Deery's statement and made a number of arrests, but it was soon revealed as a tissue of lies. There were no footprints of the alleged mob around the body, and the informer was unable to lead the police to the murder site when asked. Despite an intensive search no trace could be found of a Bradley in the district, whilst one of the men accused by Deery of an earlier assault had an unassailable alibi. The Crown Solicitor rejected Deery's allegations and he was later convicted of perjury, receiving a seven-year sentence. Deery was the only person to be gaoled in connection with Murray's murder. With the collapse of his credibility, the police inquiry petered out. The suspects arrested on his word were released, and nobody ever stood trial for the murder.

If neither the tenants of Derryveagh nor a Ribbonman terrorist killed James Murray, who was behind his assassination? According to a novel published in the United States by a Derryveagh emigrant some years later, Adair himself ordered it, so he would have an excuse to evict his tenants! A more likely theory, which was finally favoured by the RIC (although they could not prove it), stated that the murder was the plan of a Scottish shepherd by the name of Dougal Rankin, acting in collusion with the dead man's wife. This woman was apparently having an affair with Rankin, who lodged in the house. Another shepherd, Adam Grierson, reported he caught them kissing in the kitchen one afternoon, only a few weeks before the murder. It has been suggested that Rankin tampered with Murray's revolver, which was only fired once because the cylinder was improperly loaded. This was to give the impression Murray was trapped by hostile tenants after his weapon jammed, rather than caught unawares by somebody he trusted. The police believed the actual murder was the act of a third shepherd, Archibald Campbell, carried out on Rankin's orders. The two men were close friends, and gave each other alibis for the day of the killing. It was to Dougal Rankin that J. F. Maguire, the Member of Parliament for Donegal, referred in the House of Commons, when condemning the Derryveagh evictions in 1861: 'There was one man in Donegal who was openly suspected of the crime. Whether he was guilty or not was a matter between God and himself, but it was a curious fact that this man wore the dead man's clothing at his funeral and that he was extremely intimate with the man's wife.'

Any doubts about who killed James Murray did not deter John George Adair from evicting the tenants of Derryveagh. On 8 April, his bailiffs, protected by two hundred policemen, began clearing the estate. Within a week nearly two hundred and fifty people had been removed, and thirty houses destroyed. About one in five of those made homeless were allowed to return on new leases, but most of the rest emigrated from Ireland to the United States, where they settled in the city of Baltimore. The Derryveagh evictions did not put an end to unrest in the area, and Adair's turbulent shepherds continued to commit acts of violence. In March 1861, Dougal Rankin shot and wounded a policeman during a tavern brawl in Strabane, County Tyrone. He was sent to goal for two years. In the same year, Adam Grierson, Murray's successor as steward, got into trouble with the law after he shot one tenant and beat another up.

Grierson – 'a Scotchman of a very low class . . . drunken and restless' as one contemporary commentator described him – was dismissed without a reference from Adair's service in 1862, possibly for embezzling money from his employer. He planned to emigrate, but in April 1863 was ambushed close to his cottage in Derryveagh and shot. Before dying he was said to have told a bystander that his murderer was Francis Bradley, the son of an evicted tenant. The friends and relatives of the young man disputed the statement, and swore he was the victim of false testimony. After three successive trials, in each of which the jury could not agree on a verdict, the charges against Bradley were dropped. There were no further disturbances on the Derryveagh estate, possibly because the majority of its inhabitants were now in the United States. In other parts of Ireland and Donegal, however, acts of sabotage and boycotts continued until after 1880, when a series of Land Acts finally put an end to the recurring war between tenants and their landlords.

In later years, John George Adair built a magnificent mock castle called Glenveagh on his estate. He became a very wealthy man through his ruthless exploitation of the land he purchased, and died in St Louis, Missouri, in

1882. His American widow sold off most of the extensive Adair properties, but the Glenveagh Estate (as it was now known) remained in the family until 1938. Then it was purchased by Henry McIllhenny, an American millionaire who was descended from one of the Derryveagh tenants evicted by Adair. He maintained the castle, and planted the magnificent gardens for which the estate is now world-famous. Glenveagh is now a national park, and the visitor may freely roam the starkly beautiful hillsides and valley where Murray and Grierson were murdered nearly one hundred and fifty years ago.

THE NEWTOWNSTEWART
BANK MURDER

When a judge calls a murder 'the most extraordinary case ever tried in this or any other country', one can be sure that a remarkable crime has taken place. The same judge's description of the man standing in the dock before him will confirm this impression. 'He is not a common cut-throat or robber. He is a gentleman filling the position of an officer in one of the Queen's most honourable services; he is in fact the Sub-Inspector of Police in charge of that District.' The atrocity that led to these comments took place in the small Ulster town of Newtownstewart, County Tyrone, during the reign of Queen Victoria. Even though the police were sure they had caught the culprit within three days of the killing, he was such an unlikely suspect that no jury wanted to declare him guilty. The accused man stood trial for his alleged crime on no less than three occasions, making him the hardest murderer to convict in Irish legal history.

At 4 p.m. on the afternoon of 29 June 1871, a serving girl at the Northern Banking Company building in Newtownstewart was shocked to discover the bloody body of William Glass, the assistant manager, on the premises. He lay dead on the floor of the bank's private office, which was adjacent to the room used for dealings with the public. A copper file had been driven through the brain from ear to ear, and there were a number of deep gashes on his face and head. William Glass was stretched out beside an open safe, from which the bank's deposits of gold and bank notes had disappeared. There were no signs that the dead man had struggled to fight off the attack, indicating that a trusted acquaintance rather than a stranger had murdered him.

The police were called immediately, and the local Royal Irish Constabulary (RIC) District Inspector T. H. Montgomery arrived at the bank. To the surprise of everybody on the scene, his first suggestion was that Glass had committed suicide. When bystanders pointed out the victim was unlikely to have hacked himself to death, he abandoned this theory and ordered a search of the town and its surroundings. After telegraphing his RIC counterparts in other parts of Ulster, Montgomery joined the hunt for the unknown killer until about midnight, when he said he was going home to get a few hours' sleep. Instead he went to an area on the outskirts of Newtownstewart known as Grangewood, where at two in the morning he chanced to meet Inspector W. F. Purcell of Omagh, who was coming to help with the murder inquiry. Montgomery explained he was keeping a watch on the property of the Great Northern Railway in the neighbourhood, which the company had warned him might be sabotaged by strikers. The two policemen walked back into the town together, and discussed the murder. During the course of the conversation Montgomery asked Purcell whether he thought 'a person seen coming out of the bank after the murder could be convicted if he had no blood on his clothes.'

His motive for raising this odd question was made apparent on the following day. Several witnesses had seen the RIC inspector in the Northern Banking Company around the supposed time of Glass's murder. The living quarters of the branch manager, Mr Grahame, whose sister Mrs

Thomson was staying with him, were adjacent to the commercial offices. At 2.30 p.m., Montgomery knocked on the kitchen door to ask if Mr Grahame would like to come fishing on the next Saturday. Miss Thomson answered, and told him that her brother worked at a sub-branch of the bank on Thursdays, and was never home before 7 p.m. Montgomery went away after a few minutes, but other statements indicated he had been on the premises for at least thirty minutes before and after this brief call. A woman customer remembered hearing Glass talking with a male visitor in the inner office around 2 p.m., although she did not see the person. And shortly after 3 p.m., Mary Anne Comers, an assistant in a shop on the other side of the street, noticed the RIC inspector stick his head out of the front door of the bank, and then go back in again. A few minutes later, the door opened again and she saw him hurry out of the building.

Every fact and clue gathered in the inquiry pointed suspicion at one man – and incredibly it was one of the RIC officers investigating the case. On the face of it, T. H. Montgomery seemed an extremely improbable bank robber. With his good looks, immaculate grooming and well-tailored suits, he seemed to epitomize the ideal of a dedicated young policeman. His superiors in the RIC thought him capable of rising to the senior ranks of the force. Montgomery, the scion of a respected Ulster family, had transferred to Newtownstewart so his wife could be near her father, a clergyman and theologian. It was hard for his colleagues to accept that this paragon could suddenly turn to murder and robbery, yet the evidence against him was so strong it could not be ignored. Montgomery had been a bank clerk before joining the police force, and was friendly with both the bank manager, Mr Grahame, and his assistant,

William Glass, whom he was helping study for the entrance examination to the RIC. Montgomery was familiar with the routines at the bank, and knew about the comings and goings of its two staff members. Mr Grahame recalled a particularly significant conversation with the suspect a few weeks previously. One day, Montgomery mentioned that there seemed to be nothing that would stop a thief walking in and robbing the bank. By way of a reply, Grahame took out his pistol, and swore he would shoot anybody who tried. Montgomery knew that the bank mnager would be away on Thursday, when the unarmed Glass was alone in the bank office.

Three days later, Montgomery was charged with robbery and murder. He declared a mistake had been made and seemed unconcerned at the accusation. A trial date was set after the initial hearing, and then put back to allow the police to make further inquiries. Some months later, a young boy hunting rabbits in Grangewood, the spot where Montgomery had met Sub-Inspector Purcell on the night of the murder, discovered £1,500 in notes and some gold hidden beneath a stone in the forest. The cache was identified as the loot from the Northern Banking Company robbery. A billhook was uncovered a few dozen yards away. This weapon had its socket weighted with lead, and its blade matched the deep slash marks on the face and body of the murdered man.

A gunsmith named John McDonnell revealed Montgomery had purchased a quantity of lead from him shortly before the murder, supposedly to make bullets for his pistol. When his home was searched there was no sign of the metal, and the police found none of the moulds used for making the bullets. They decided Montgomery's sole purpose in buying the missing lead was to fabricate the murder weapon.

The first of the epic series of trials that eventually convicted Montgomery took place in Omagh in 1872. A known
criminal, or even an ordinary working man, standing in
the dock with so much evidence against him, might have
expected to be convicted and hung in short shrift. But
Montgomery was not like most people who commit such
crimes. He was a pillar of respectability and a high-ranking
police officer – not the sort of man anybody would expect to
be accused of premeditated murder. It was difficult for some
jury members to accept that this trusted shepherd was really
a ravenous wolf, and perhaps they placed undue emphasis on
any points raised in Montgomery's favour by his barrister.

The prosecution brought circumstantial evidence to place
Montgomery in the bank at the time of the murder, whilst
witnesses testified to earlier conversations that suggested
he had been planning the robbery for some time. Nobody
in the bank had seen any blood on the overcoat or clothes
of the accused, but a police expert demonstrated how
Montgomery could have stabbed and pierced Glass without
being splashed. The RIC inspector was well on the way to
being found guilty, when a dubious legal decision went in
his favour. Judge Lawson, presiding over the case, refused
to allow the prosecuting counsel to introduce evidence about
Montgomery's desperate financial situation. His defending
counsel, the famous Irish barrister, MacDonagh QC, seized
on the apparent failure of the prosecution to explain why
a respected policeman had suddenly turned into a thief
and murderer. His closing argument, in which he stressed
Montgomery had no impelling motive for the murder, in-
fluenced a minority of the jury. They could not agree on a
verdict, and split into nine for conviction and three against.
Montgomery was ordered to be tried again.

In reality, the RIC inspector was in serious trouble over money, due to a number of reckless business investments. He was heavily in debt to his father-in-law, and had embezzled several hundred pounds given to him by two of his police constables. Montgomery was in danger of being dismissed from the RIC, and facing fraud charges, if he could not replace these sums. The judge at his second trial – which pitted MacDonagh QC against his great rival, Sergeant Armstrong (appearing for the Crown) – admitted this incriminating information into evidence. The barrister for the defence responded by asking how Montgomery could have walked out of the bank carrying a large wad of currency and a heavy weapon, without one witness noticing it. Two members of the jury agreed with this valid point, and a second retrial was arranged.

Sergeant Armstrong rebutted this suggestion at Montgomery's third trial by a simple but very effective demonstration. He stood a police officer, of about the same build as the accused man and wearing his clothes, upon a table in the courtroom. Armstrong then revealed how the officer had the stolen money and murder weapon disposed about his person, completely unnoticeable to a casual observer's eye. This time it took the jury less than an hour and a half to bring in a verdict of guilty. Before receiving his sentence, Montgomery was allowed to address the court. At this late stage, he decided to confess to killing Glass, but claimed he should not receive the death penalty because he was insane at the time. According to his story he had been 'drugged and poisoned' by his wife's father some months previously, which had affected his reason. As a result, he had developed a 'monomania for robbing banks' and was unable to stop himself killing Glass. This attempt to wriggle out of paying the full price for a cold-blooded murder moved nobody in the courtroom, and Montgomery was condemned to death.

In the weeks preceding the execution, he cleared up several confusing minor details about the murder, whilst clinging on to his pretence of insanity in the vain hope of gaining a reprieve. The most surprising point concerned the time of the killing of Glass, which he stated was at 2.30 p.m. rather than after 3 p.m. as the police had thought. Montgomery remarked that his hands and clothes were covered in blood whilst he was speaking to Miss Thomson, which he then sponged off before leaving the bank. When describing the murder to a journalist shortly before going to the gallows, the RIC inspector revealed a chilling lack of remorse for his victim. 'Poor Glass didn't speak at all after he was struck. He had an easy time of it.'

THE MAAMTRASNA MASSACRE

On the morning of 18 August 1882, in the district of Maamtrasna (then in County Galway, today in County Mayo), one of the neighbours of John Joyce of Boithrin a tSleibhe made a terrible discovery. Visiting the man's tiny cottage to borrow some thread, he stumbled upon a scene of utter carnage. The only door had been torn from its hinges, and the entire Joyce family lay dead or dying inside. John Joyce, his mother, wife and daughter had been bludgeoned or shot to death, whilst his teenage sons Michael and Patrick were gravely wounded. Two dogs had entered the cottage and were eating the arm of old Mrs Joyce, the matriarch of the family. Thus began one of the most controversial episodes in the nineteenth-century Irish land wars.

Maamtrasna lies just to the west of Lough Mask, and is one of the most wildly beautiful areas in the west of Ireland. In 1882, it was mainly Gaelic-speaking, and thinly inhabited by various descendants of the Joyce and O'Casey clans. Living standards were low, and there was great poverty in the small stone cottages and cabins scattered along the glens and mountain slopes. At this time the longstanding feud between Irish tenants and their landlords was reaching its climax, and assassinations, riots and evictions were common occurrences. The local contingent of the Royal Irish Constabulary (RIC), when they were informed of the massacre, assumed it was another incident

34

in these disturbances, albeit one of the most sensational to be recorded.

John Joyce's cottage was a primitive thatched stone and earth dwelling, without even a chimney. Inside it consisted of a large room with a kitchen at one end and a barn for the owner's cows at the other; a recessed alcove in one of the kitchen walls contained a bed where John Joyce slept with his wife, Margaret. Another narrow room held a bed that was shared by his eighty-year-old mother and her three grandchildren. The assassins had entered the unlocked cottage in the early hours of the morning, and first murdered John Joyce and his wife in the alcove. They had then gone into the other room and attacked his mother and children as they lay sleeping in their shared bed. The entire attack was over in less than five minutes. The two survivors were very badly injured. Michael Joyce had received two bullet wounds, and died that afternoon after giving his account of the savage assault. His younger brother, Patrick, was battered around the head and face; he could remember nothing, having been knocked unconscious as he slept.

When they tried to question people in the area the RIC were met by a wall of silence. Policemen were considered the lackeys of the landlords and the English government, and it was rumoured that John Joyce was their local informer. RIC men were often seen visiting his cottage or chatting to him and his family on the roadside. Many of the inhabitants of Maamtrasna were disgusted by the killings, yet they were afraid to cross the men behind it. The RIC, who were under pressure from their superiors and the press to solve the case rapidly, could do little more than 'round up the usual suspects'. They arrested a farmer named Big John Casey, who was known to have a grudge against John Joyce. There was nothing tangible to connect him to the slaughter and he was released within a couple of hours. By the fourth day after the killings the inquiry into the massacre seemed to be getting nowhere. Then ten men from Maamtrasna and its vicinity were suddenly arrested and charged with murder.

It transpired that three witnesses had come forward to testify. They had seen the killings and could identify the culprits. Anthony Joyce, their leader, brother of the murdered John, said that he was woken up in his cottage on the night of the murder by the barking of his dogs, and saw some shadowy figures passing along the road. Realizing that they were up to no good, he took a short cut across the fields to his brother's house. Accompanied by this man and his son, he followed the gang for several miles, until they came to John Joyce's cottage. Anthony Joyce and his relatives hid in some bushes, and watched as the ten men went inside and attacked the sleeping victims with clubs and revolvers. Anthony Joyce listed the names of the killers, all of whom were from Maamtrasna and known to him personally.

It should be said at once that this was an extremely unlikely story; in fact most of it was obviously a pack of lies. The informers stated that they had been able to follow and recognize the ten men in the dark, whilst staying back far enough not to be seen. Yet Michael Joyce, when asked to identify his killers on his deathbed, said they had blackened their faces and he could not name any of them. If one of the victims was unable to recognize his murderers from a few feet away, how could the alleged witness do so from many yards distance at night? Five of those named by Anthony Joyce were certainly involved in the Maamtrasna massacre, so he had some knowledge of who committed the crime.

Nonetheless he also accused five men who had nothing to do it. His motive for framing some of his neighbours may be attributed to a mixture of greed and spite. The informer and his accomplices received rewards amounting to over £1,200, in addition to which they had the satisfaction of paying off some old scores against their enemies. There was a long-running feud between the Maolra Joyces, Anthony's branch of the family, and their cousins the Shaun Joyces. It was hardly coincidence that four Shaun Joyces were amongst the accused.

The police, under orders to solve the murders at any cost, were more interested in securing convictions than establishing whether their suspects were guilty or innocent. They welcomed the three Maolra Joyces with open arms, and cared little about the accuracy of their testimony as long as it stood up in court. 'The three independent and irreproachable witnesses', as the newspapers called them, were whisked away for safekeeping whilst the authorities prepared prosecutions against the ten men. The Maamtrasna prisoners were moved to Dublin, where a jury of city dwellers could be expected to have less sympathy for the alleged murderers. On 1 November 1882, they were brought to the old courthouse at Green Street to answer the cases against them.

The Maamtrasna ten were given what today would be called a 'show trial'. The murders had outraged the public, and the government was under pressure to make an example of the perpetrators. The feeling against the Maamtrasna ten was so strong that their solicitor had grave difficulty finding a barrister willing to defend them. The presiding judge, the Right Hon. Justice Barry, was clearly biased towards the prosecution, adding to the problems already facing the men in the dock. Most of them could not speak English, and although interpreters were present, had great difficulty in following the proceedings. The evidence against them was flimsy, and based mainly on the dubious 'eyewitness' accounts of the Maolra Joyces, supplemented by the unsupported testimony of witnesses who 'overheard' the murders being planned. The prosecution strengthened its weak case by persuading two of the accused, Anthony Philbin and Thomas Casey, to turn state's evidence and testify against the others. In return for betraying their co-accused, they were promised a free pardon.

The remaining eight prisoners were to be tried one by one. In other circumstances, this method might have favoured the five innocent men amongst them, but in fact it helped the prosecution. The order of the trials was selected so that the two most obviously guilty prisoners would be judged first, leaving a residue of prejudice against the others when it came to their turn. Each case was to follow directly after the one before. Patrick Joyce, the first man up, was found guilty in eight minutes by the jury. Patrick Casey, the next to stand trial, was convicted within twelve minutes. Both were sentenced to death. These two had, in fact, been part of the gang that murdered John Joyce and his family. However, the third prisoner to face the court took no part in the massacre, and became the victim of a cruel miscarriage of justice. Myles Doyle, a fierce-looking bearded man, was in his mid-forties at the time of the trial. His outlaw's face was deceptive of his true character, and he was a highly respected member of the Shaun branch of the Joyces of Maamtrasna. Myles Joyce had been at home in bed with his wife on the night of the killings. But he was a particular enemy of Anthony Joyce, who had vindictively included his name on his inventory of the Maamtrasna killers. Philbin and Casey, whose freedom depended on convicting their fellow prisoners, corroborated the testimony of the three Maolra Joyces against their cousin. These statements might have been rejected in another courtroom as unreliable, but in this prejudiced atmosphere they were accepted at face value. At the conclusion of the trial, Myles Doyle was declared guilty in eight minutes.

What happened next must be considered one of the most poignant moments in any Irish trial. Myles Doyle spoke little or no English, and had sat silently throughout the proceedings, with his head bowed. But when Judge Barry, as was customary, asked if he had anything to say before his sentence was passed, the sullen man in the dock suddenly became animated. Myles Doyle burst out with a torrent of Irish, and his fervent intensity and evident passion moved even those who could not understand a word of what he was saying. The court interpreter translated the rushing torrent of language as best he could. 'He says that by the God and the Blessed Virgin above him that he had no dealings with it any more than the person who was never born, that against anyone for the last twenty years he never did any harm, and if he did that he may never go to heaven, that he is as clear of it as the child not yet born, that on the night of the murder he slept in his bed with his wife, and that he has no knowledge about it whatever. He says he is quite content with whatever the gentlemen may do with him and that whether he is hanged or crucified, he is as clear and as free as can be.'

His extraordinary declaration of innocence failed to deter Judge Barry from handing out the inevitable death penalty.

But it may have had some beneficial effect on the fates of the five men still awaiting their trials. For the Crown Solicitor, having secured three death penalties, was willing to commute the sentences of the remaining prisoners to life imprisonment, provided all agreed to plead guilty. At first the four innocent men would not agree to this compromise, and his offer was refused. Henry Concannon, their solicitor, believing it was the only hope of saving their lives, asked them to reconsider. The prisoners consulted with their parish priest, Father McHugh, and reluctantly accepted. The next trial, that of an older man named Michael Casey, had already commenced. It was halted, and the five accused men went into the dock together to plead guilty to the charges against them. All received the mandatory death penalty for murder, with a strong recommendation of mercy from the presiding judge. Some weeks afterwards they were given reprieves, and their sentences commuted to life imprisonment.

Myles Doyle had many sympathizers, but there was little hope he would be pardoned, despite efforts to establish his innocence. He was hanged along with Patrick Joyce and Patrick Casey on 15 December 1882, on a huge scaffold originally designed to take all eight of the Maamtrasna prisoners.

The execution was a messy business. Within a few years, the procedure of hanging a man would be scientifically regulated, with tables of weights and drops to ensure a quick, painless death. And from 1896 onwards there were no more triple executions held in England, after an assistant executioner accidentally fell down the trap with the condemned men. These improvements would come too late to help Myles Doyle, whose executioner, William Marwood, belonged to the rough and ready school of hangmen. Marwood botched the hanging, and Doyle was left dangling in agony for several minutes whilst the men on the scaffold shook and pulled the rope to try and break his neck.

The injustice done to the four innocent Maamtrasna prisoners serving a life sentence was not forgotten. Over the following years, there were a number of attempts to have their cases re-opened. Requests to pardon or re-try the men were ignored by the British government, even after two of them died in prison. It was 1902 before the three surviving prisoners, all members of the Shaun branch of the Joyces, were released and allowed to return to the remote valley from which they had been so unjustly removed.

The motive for the slaughter at John Joyce's cottage in 1882 is still shrouded in mystery. According to one local tradition it may be traced back to a Fenian atrocity that took place in January of that year, when a land agent named Joseph Huddy and his grandson were murdered and thrown into Mask Lough. After their bodies were unexpectedly discovered by the RIC, the region was rife with rumours that an informer had tipped them off. It was said that an old woman, who had been watching from a hillside, told the police where the bodies were hidden for a reward. According to one legend, the informer was the mother of John Joyce, who brought down the wrath of the killers of the Huddys on her son and his household.

A more likely explanation, which was supported by the accounts of some of those involved, claims the killings were planned by Big John Casey, the farmer briefly arrested by the RIC in its aftermath. John Joyce, a notorious sheep thief, had provoked his well-off neighbour by preying on his flocks once too often. Casey decided it was time to put

41

a permanent end to these activities, and organized a raiding party to attack the victims' cottage. The target of the attack was John Joyce rather than his family, but the raiding party had consumed large quantities of poiteen and butchered the entire family in a drunken rage.

THE TIPPERARY FAIRY MURDER

When a person takes another's life it is usually for some surprisingly banal motive. No matter how appalling in their detail, most murders spring from the common vices of greed, lust, anger and jealousy. The so-called 'Tipperary fairy murder' is a rare example of a homicide that was not simply an extreme form of everyday human behaviour. Fuelled by strange beliefs in magical forces, and carried out against a background of communal ignorance and superstition, it seems more akin to a medieval witch burning than a modern crime. Yet its bizarre details hide a familiar story that has provoked many murders over the ages.

The Irish phenomenon of 'fairy killings' has its origins in traditional peasant beliefs that date back several thousand years. In Ireland, fairies were the supernatural 'little people', who shared the land with ordinary human beings. Fairies were very dangerous to offend, and interfering with their standing stones or 'fairy rings' (in reality the banks of prehistoric forts) could bring a variety of retributions: a man's cattle might fall sick or his crops fail; a member of his family could be injured. Worst of all, the invisible fairies stole away children and young women, leaving behind unhealthy replicas of their victims, who looked the same but were actually 'changelings'. The activities of fairies explained the birth of infants with physical or mental disabilities, and the onset of sudden diseases in children and adults. When such tragedies occurred, they were interpreted as the result of the healthy person being replaced by a changeling. The 'fairy-struck' victim could only be restored to health by driving the changeling away. This was best achieved with the help of a 'fairy doctor', who could call on spells, potions and rituals. Some fairy doctors were genuine healers, who treated their patients with well-tried herbal remedies. Many others were superstitious quacks, who bullied and tortured the sick people they were supposed to be helping.

The most extreme method of getting rid of a fairy changeling was to kill it. The murders of several children who were thought to be changelings are recorded in the nineteenth century. In 1888, one such incident took place near Killarney in County Kerry, when a woman named Joanna Doyle murdered her retarded twelve-year-old son Patsy with an axe because 'he was not my son, he was a devil, a bad fairy.' There were many others like Patsy Doyle during that era, children whose physical and mental disabilities led to them being culled from the population with the justification that they were not human at all. The killing of adults on the pretext that they were changelings was a much less common occurrence. In 1895, however, Irish newspaper readers were shocked by sensational reports that a husband had brutally murdered his sick wife for this very reason. As the nightmarish details of the crime emerged, it seemed to have slipped out of the pages of the Tales of the Brothers Grimm, or from some explorer's description of primitive tribes in the interior of Africa or South America.

Bridget Cleary, the victim of the crime, lived with her husband Michael and aged father in the townland of

Ballyvadlea, County Tipperary. Although within site of the haunted mountain of Slievenamon, notorious in Irish folklore as the haunt of fairies and other spirits, the area was mainly English-speaking and quite near to the busy towns of Clonmel and Fethard. Bridget Cleary came from local stock, but neither she nor her husband resembled the stereotype of the ignorant Irish peasant portrayed in Punch and other English magazines of the Victorian era. The couple pursued good trades, and both husband and wife were literate and ambitious. Nor did they live in a thatched mud-walled cabin like most people of their class. Their home was a well-built slate-roofed cottage of the type local authorities had recently begun erecting in rural areas, without sewage or running water yet far superior to the houses of most of their neighbours.

In 1895, Michael Cleary was in his mid-thirties, and plied his trade of cooper or barrel-maker from his own workshop. Born in the nearby town of Killenaule, he had met his future wife, Bridget, in Clonmel about ten years previously. The couple married in 1887 and she returned to Ballyvadlea to look after her sick mother, whilst her husband remained in Clonmel for some years to save money for his own premises. Bridget Cleary was twenty-six years old at the time of her death. Her main occupation was as a self-employed dressmaker, but she supplemented the household income by keeping hens and selling their eggs. Independent and strong-willed, she was by no means a typical 'shawlie', as city people called the women of the rural poor because of the black shawls they wore. The pretty and comparatively well-dressed woman seems to have stood out amongst her peers and been resented for it. There was some gossip locally about the couple's friendship with their Protestant neighbours, William and Mary Simpson, who were living on lands taken from evicted Catholic tenants. Whilst this may have marked the rising social status of the cooper and his wife, it offended many in the community. Some whispered that Bridget and William Simpson were lovers, which contributed to the ill feeling already caused by her general air of superiority.

Bridget Cleary had a reputation for being difficult and highly strung; she was also childless after eight years of marriage. These facts may have caused some stress in her relationship with her husband, but the couple seemed happy enough until early March 1895. Then Bridget caught a cold whilst out walking with her husband one day, which quickly developed into a fever and severe head pains. Her condition worsened over the next few days. On 9 March, her husband went to Fethard and asked the local dispensary doctor, William Crean, to attend her. Crean, despite further requests from Michael Cleary, did not call on Bridget until the morning of 13 March, and he appears to have been drunk during the consultation. He left some medicine but it was not given to the sick woman, possibly because her husband had no faith in the doctor's competence. Later that afternoon. Father Cornelius Ryan, a local priest, gave her the last rites, since she appeared to be in some danger of dying.

Michael Cleary, frantic with worry after the doctor's failure to help his wife, now turned his back on orthodox medicine. He visited an old woman who sold herbal cures, and purchased a magic potion called 'the seventh' because it was blessed by the hands of the seventh son of a seventh son. On the evening of 13 March, he administered the potion with the help of one Jack Dunne, an older man steeped in fairy lore and superstitions. Dunne bore a great deal of responsibility for the tragedy that was to follow, as he informed Cleary that the patient was not his wife but a fairy changeling. He said that the old woman's potion was of no use, and recommended that he go to Dennis Ganey, a well-known fairy-doctor who lived some miles away. The husband accepted this advice and hurried off to the doctor on the following day, returning with a concoction of herbs and instructions on how to administer it.

When Cleary got home from the herb doctor, some shocking news was waiting for him. He found out that his father had died, and the wake would be taking place that night. There were few events as important as this in rural life, but Cleary decided that he could not go. Doyle had warned him that if the fairy was not banished by midnight his real wife would be lost forever. As the time to administer the herbs grew closer, his inability to attend the wake must have added to his anger towards Bridget over the trouble her sickness was causing.

Night fell and Jack Dunne arrived at the cottage to oversee the driving out of the changeling. Bridget's aunt, Mary Kennedy, and her four cousins were waiting in the kitchen, along with a couple of other visitors. Eleven people were involved in what now took place, including Bridget's own father, Patrick Boland. First a pail of new milk was brought to the house, and the herbs (gathered from potent healing plants like St John's Wort, foxglove and henbane) were steeped and boiled. Next Bridget's cousins pinned her to the bed, while Jack Dunne and Michael Cleary tried to force her to drink the bitter infusion. She refused, but her husband pushed it into her mouth on a spoon, and held his hand over her face to make sure it went down. He then told his wife to swear on the name of God that she was the real Bridget Cleary – a ritual that was constantly repeated throughout the evening.

William Simpson and his wife, who came to visit her that evening, witnessed the indignities inflicted on the unwilling patient. A poker was heated in the fire, and, when red-hot, waved in her face to invoke the traditional fairy fear of iron and fire. A pail of urine was thrown on the sick woman, soaking her body and nightdress. Her cousins lifted her off the bed by the limbs, and began violently shaking and tossing her in the air. All the while, she was cursed as a fairy and told to go back where she came from. Towards midnight, Bridget Cleary was forced to endure one more terrifying experience. She was brought to the wide chimney, lifted over the fire on her back, and held there until her nightdress began smouldering around her buttocks. She was again made to swear she was the real Bridget Cleary. By now she was reduced to a hysterical wreck, and Cleary and Doyle relented and put her back to bed. Mary Kennedy bathed her burnt buttocks and changed the scorched nightdress, afterwards consoling her niece as best she could. At length, Bridget Cleary calmed down and fell asleep.

Although unbelievably harsh, fairy doctoring could be crudely effective as a medical treatment. Irish peasants often called the herbal mixture used by fairy-healers 'blast', a fair description of its botanical strength. Many of the ingredients had powerful healing qualities on a variety of diseases, both physical and psychological, whilst the shaking and heating of the body might help expel fevers or ease muscular problems. Yet the violence displayed towards Bridget Cleary was excessive. The presence of William Simpson may well have had something to do with this. There must be a suspicion that the victim's cousins took the opportunity to humiliate her in front of a suspected lover. Whatever happened that evening unleashed demons in the mind of Michael Cleary. His obsessive delusion about his 'changeling' wife would shortly have a disastrous consequence.

On the following morning, Thursday 15 March 1895, the patient was much improved, and Cleary asked Father Ryan to call and say Mass. The priest noted that Bridget was more coherent than on his previous visit, although she appeared nervous and wild-eyed. Afterwards she was able to get out of bed and hold conversations with some of her visitors, later getting dressed for the first time since the illness began. Not surprisingly, Bridget was more than a little displeased with her husband after his rough treatment, and during the evening mocked his half-voiced suspicions that she was still a changeling. It was a fatal mistake for her to make. The bitter argument that developed reached its climax around midnight, when the couple sat down at the kitchen table to share a pot of tea with their relatives and friends.

There were eight or nine people in the cottage, most of whom witnessed what happened next. Michael Cleary demanded that his wife eat three pieces of bread before she drank any tea, swearing after each that she was the real Bridget Cleary. Bridget submitted and ate the first two pieces, but refused to take the third because her throat was too dry. Cleary, berserk with rage, threw her to the ground and forced the third piece of bread into her mouth. Nobody in the kitchen intervened. He stripped off her outer clothes until she was in her shift, and grabbed a lighted stick from the fire. Waving it in his wife's face, he again told her to swallow the bread and swear she was Bridget Cleary. When she could not get it down he set fire to her chemise. The flames began to engulf her, and to the horror of those watching he grabbed a lamp and poured oil over her writhing body. Bridget Cleary erupted into a ball of fire that sent its tendrils shooting around the room.

Mary Kennedy now tried to intervene and Cleary roughly pushed her away. When other people in the kitchen began protesting, he locked the cottage door, and took a knife from his pocket. The spectators fled into the bedroom, leaving the killer pouring more oil on the smouldering body. When it was reduced to a charred shell he went out, leaving the witnesses to the crime trapped in the cottage. After digging a shallow grave in a narrow lane about three quarters of a mile away, he came back and forced one of Bridget's cousins to help him move and bury the remains. When he returned from this second excursion it was 5 a.m. and the prisoners begged to be released. Before letting them go, Cleary extorted a promise at knifepoint that nobody would inform on him.

With so many witnesses, it was hardly surprising that the news of Bridget Cleary's burning was common knowledge within hours. The RIC were aware of her disappearance by the evening of the following day. They began gathering statements from witnesses, including John Simpson and Joanna Burke, a local woman who agreed to inform if she was not prosecuted for her involvement in the crime. Michael Cleary, meanwhile, clung on to the fading hope that his wife would now be miraculously returned by the fairies. For three nights after her death, he kept vigil beside a ring fort on the nearby hill of Kylenagranagh, accompanied by a number of his friends. In his hand, he held a black-handled knife, so that when Bridget reappeared on a grey horse he could cut her bonds and release her from the spell. But he waited in vain, and, five days after the killing, Michael Cleary and eight others were arrested and charged with murder. The following day, the charred body of Bridget Cleary was discovered in its secret grave.

In July 1895, Michael Cleary was convicted for the manslaughter of Bridget Cleary and sentenced to life imprisonment. Six men, including Bridget's father, Patrick Boland, and one woman were found guilty of wounding her, receiving sentences ranging from six months up to five years. The 'witch-burning case' (as contemporary newspapers called it) has few modern parallels in Western countries. At his trial, Cleary blamed the death of his wife on the malevolent influence of Jack Dunne, who was the chief instigator of the witch doctoring. He had strong reasons for making this accusation. Nevertheless, his explosion of rage on the night of the murder was provoked by nothing more than Bridget's refusal to eat a piece of dry bread. Stripped of its supernatural trappings, his behaviour was an extreme example of domestic violence, justified in his mind by the right to establish control over a disobedient wife. In the final analysis, his 'bad fairies' were the age-old seeds of discord that have poisoned many a marriage, often with fatal results for one or other of its partners.

Michael Cleary spent fifteen years in prison, afterwards going to England where he lived anonymously until his death. The circumstances surrounding Bridget Cleary's death passed into the folklore of the region, to be embellished with details that reinforced belief in the malevolent power of the fairies of Slievenamon. The old superstitions are respected in country areas, and even today most farmers do not interfere with the fairy rings or standing stones in their fields. One small detail about the burning of Bridget Cleary suggests this is not as foolish as it might sound. The local authority cottage where the doomed couple lived was built on a fairy fort, and had come into their possession after its previous tenants were driven out by ghostly noises in the night.

THE RATHMORE MURDER

The murder of a young Kerry woman in 1931 would later result in the giving of some of the most questionable police evidence ever heard in an Irish court. At this time, the Garda Síochána, or civic guards as they were then known, were still in their infancy. Their standards were not as high as they later became, and they were sometimes unscrupulous in their efforts to convict suspects they knew were guilty. The judge at the trial of the man accused of the Cork murder stated that he believed policemen would not tell lies. Perhaps this is nearly always true, but in this case officers may have perjured themselves, and planted a piece of false evidence in the accused man's home. It is easy to pour scorn on such tactics, but the suspect was a dangerous sex killer, and there was little doubt he had committed murder. If bad means were used to help convict him, it was towards the good end of protecting the public. The question that must be asked is whether it is ever right to tip the scales of justice.

Ellen O'Sullivan was twenty-four years old at the time of her murder, and lived on the family farm outside the village of Rathmore in County Kerry, just beside the Cork border. She worked in the local creamery, and was engaged to a man named Jeremiah Cronin, whom she had been seeing for several years. Like most courting couples, they reserved certain times in their busy schedules to be alone together. These included Sunday evenings, when Jeremiah would meet his fiancée in the village, and walk her home along the banks of the River Blackwater, which divides the counties of Cork and Kerry in this district. During these walks, it was Cronin's habit to leave his car with a friend, who would later meet him at a crossroads called Shinagh Cross.

On Sunday 8 February 1931, Ellen O'Sullivan went to Mass, then spent the afternoon visiting relatives. At around 6.45 p.m., she cycled down with a cousin to Rathmore and met her fiancée. They went off together along the riverside walk, with Ellen wheeling her bike and Cronin walking beside her. They exchanged greetings and a few words with a number of acquaintances, who were also out enjoying the pleasant evening. About a half hour later, Cronin said goodbye to Ellen at the track that led to her house, and returned by the way he had come to Shinagh Cross. At the crossroads, he retrieved his car from his cousin, who was accompanied by several friends.

Ellen O'Sullivan did not return home that evening. At first, her parents assumed she had been delayed for some reason, but by midnight they were getting worried. Her father went out with a lantern to look for her, but was unable to find any trace of his daughter. The next morning, the civic guards found her bike on the roadside near to the house, and initiated a search of the district. Five days passed before a man on the Cork side of the river noticed the long hair of a woman peeping out from under a furze bush. It was the body of Ellen O'Sullivan, hidden under a loose covering of branches. Her clothes had been ripped off, and she was naked from the waist down.

Ellen O'Sullivan had been subjected to an incredibly savage attack. The unknown murderer had knocked his victim off her bike on the roadway, then dragged her through a gap in a hedgerow to the river. He had pulled the half-unconscious woman across its shallow waters, then crossed one field to get to another, where he began raping her. When Ellen O'Sullivan fought back; he simultaneously beat her over the head with a stone and throttled her. An autopsy revealed that the forced sexual intercourse continued long after the victim was dead. Ellen O'Sullivan's clothes and possessions were scattered around the vicinity of her body. A book was found in two pieces in different places, whilst a belt, handkerchief and hat were in the corner of a nearby field. Some missing items of underwear and clothing were stuffed in a hole obscured by some grass, whilst a shoe turned up later beside the road. It had been in left in plain view on top of a wall for several days, before falling into the ditch where it was discovered. The victim's knickers remained missing for a month. They were uncovered in a field near to the cottage of David O'Shea and his sister, the closest neighbours of Ellen and her family. The item of underwear had been hidden in an old cart-cushion cover.

The civic guards came upon two important clues in their search of the area around the murder scene. A single black legging (a leather garment buckled around the calves to protect the bottom part of the trousers) had been discarded on a small island in the river. Not far away, in an adjacent field on the Cork bank, lay a single woollen sock of a type commonly worn by rural Irishmen. It seemed likely that the murderer had lost the footwear, probably when he was dragging his victim from the road to the field where he killed her.

It was obvious from the start of the inquiry that the murderer was a local man; a stranger would not have known the terrain well enough to find his way from the road to the remote scene of the crime. There was also an implied degree of premeditation, since the victim was brought to a quiet place some distance from where she was abducted. Ellen O'Sullivan was a big, athletic woman and weighed around ten stone. Only an exceptionally strong man could have carried his heavy victim for such a distance. The civic guards had a suspect whom they thought fitted the profile of the killer, and arrested her fiancé, Jeremiah Cronin. However, it was established that his movements after leaving the young woman could be corroborated by his friends at Shinagh Cross. After nine days, Cronin was released, and the civic guards concentrated their attention on a second suspect.

David O'Shea was a thirty-three-year-old single man, who lived with his sister Kathy in a tiny cottage near Ellen O'Sullivan's house. His mental capacity was so limited that he was almost subnormal (at his trial, his own defence counsel called him stupid). O'Shea eked out a living from the family smallholding and by occasional casual work as a farm labourer. When interviewed about his movements on the evening of the murder, he gave contradictory and improbable answers to the question put to him. O'Shea admitted he had been on the riverside walk that evening, and had passed a young couple as he headed towards Shinagh Cross. From his description it was undoubtedly his neighbour and her fiancé, but O'Shea made the unlikely claim that he did not recognize them. He said he continued walking on towards Shinagh Cross, which he reached around 7 p.m. There was nobody there, and after waiting around the crossroads for half an hour he returned home. When he got back to his cottage around 9 p.m., his sister was already fast asleep. At a later interview, the labourer claimed that he originally intended to visit his father, but changed his mind.

Both of these statements were palpably untrue. Cronin's friends were waiting at Shinagh Cross when O'Shea was supposed to be lingering there, whilst he had earlier told a neighbour he would not be calling on his father. Either the suspect did not go to Shinagh Cross at all, or he was there much later than he claimed. The civic guards believed that after passing the couple on the riverside walk, their suspect doubled back and followed them back along the path. He hid and waited until Cronin had gone off to meet his friends, then approached the victim and attacked her.

The policemen questioning David O'Shea noticed that his hands were covered in scratches. He explained he had been cutting down undergrowth. On the other hand, the investigators thought to themselves, the scratches might have come about when the farm labourer was pulling back the furze bush to hide Ellen O'Sullivan's body. The black legging found by the river provided further evidence against O'Shea. Several people stated that he had owned a pair, and worn them on Sundays instead of his usual brown leggings. The suspect insisted that he possessed only the brown pair, but blackened them with boot polish to go to Mass. The civic guards examined the brown leggings and asked why there were no traces of bootblack on them; O'Shea replied he had not polished them for months. But an observant neighbour remembered recently seeing O'Shea wearing black leggings at a dance, and recalled that one of them was damaged and had a rib pointing out of the leather. When shown the legging found on the island in the river, which had the same defect, he identified it as the one worn by the suspect. Further inquiries revealed a cobbler in the town had repaired a black leather legging for O'Shea in the past.

The civic guards searched the cottage and found some cushion stuffing under a pile of manure in the yard. It resembled traces found in the cover containing Ellen O'Sullivan's knickers. Everything pointed towards David O'Shea as the murderer, yet there was not enough evidence to be sure of convicting him. In 1931, the police did not have the advantages of modern techniques like DNA testing, which could have identified O'Shea as the killer through his semen. In order to ensure a conviction, the civic guards needed his confession or, failing that, a witness who could testify to overhearing the suspect implicate himself in the murder of Ellen O'Sullivan.

The necessary verbal evidence was acquired under the most debatable circumstances. According to the police at O'Shea's trial, they planted the human equivalent of an electronic 'bug' in his cottage to eavesdrop on his conversations with his sister. In the course of a search of their cottage by a party of five policemen, a civic guard named Keane hid himself under Kathy O'Shea's bed. The suspect and his sister, who presumably could not count beyond three, failed to notice this deception. An hour later, Keane's colleagues came back and retrieved him, after which he wrote down a full account of what he had heard the brother and sister say. The two searches were ostensibly mounted to look for the other black legging, and a match to the grey sock left near to the murder scene. During the second raid the sock was discovered hidden in a disused milk tankard in David O'Shea's room. The farm labourer was taken into custody and charged with the murder of Ellen O'Sullivan.

David O'Shea's trial was held in August 1931. Civic Guard Keane's testimony played an important part in the prosecution's case, yet it is a valid question as to whether the episode he described ever actually happened. The police did not mention it to the O'Sheas at the time. Indeed the alleged discussion between the brother and sister only came to the attention of the defence when Keane repeated it on the witness stand. Their comments to each other, if his word was to be believed, suggested that David O'Shea was undeniably guilty, and showed the siblings conspiring with each other to conceal important evidence.

Civic Guard Keane's account of what he heard whilst lurking under the bed is well worth repeating from the court transcript. Firstly, the O'Sheas spoke about his other black legging, which was one of the objects the police were still searching for.

Kathy: My God, where is the legging. Did they take it?
David: See if it's behind the box. Look, quick, it's here.
Kathy: Rush, quick. Take it away quick. Burn it.

Next they explained why no dirt or river clay was found on O'Shea's trousers, which the Civic Guards had taken away with his socks for examination.

Kathy: Did I not tell you to brush your clothes when you came in that night. Wasn't it well we washed the pants?

Finally, Kathy clarified why they had not disposed of the incriminating grey sock, which was found in her brother's room during the second search.

David: What did you do with the sock?

Kathy: I was looking for it all day and I couldn't find it. My God, I must burn it if I find it.'

There are a number of points about Civic Guard Keane's testimony that lead the observer to think that these sentences were never uttered by the suspect and his sister. The most obvious concern the legging, which was the single most vital piece of evidence against the labourer. If David O'Shea had it in his hands, why did the civic guard not jump out from under the bed and stop him burning it? Five policemen were supposed to have searched the three-room cottage and been unable to find either the legging or the sock. Yet the lost sock was found in an obvious hiding place on the second search, provoking further doubts about the veracity of the police. One grey sock looks much like another, and they had already taken away David O'Shea's socks. It would have been easy to take one of these, and slip it into the milk tankard to incriminate the suspect. A forensic expert went to some lengths in the witness box to prove that this sock matched the one near the murder scene, but David O'Shea may have had several pairs of the same make and colour.

Both Kathy and David O'Shea denied the conversation attributed to them ever took place. Nevertheless their testimony in court did nothing to help his case. Kathy O'Shea swore she had not spoken of the murder to her brother at all after the first raid, which was simply unbelievable. And the answers she gave under cross-examination left the impression that she knew more than she would admit about her brother's part in the murder. The testimony of David O'Shea was riddled with lies and inconsistencies and was not that of an innocent man with nothing to hide. He denied being familiar with the area where Ellen O'Sullivan was kidnapped and murdered, even though he had lived in Rathmore all his life. His apparent ignorance of her engagement to Jeremiah Cronin, and his supposed failure to recognize the couple on the river walk, were so ridiculous that they could be discounted as lies. The admission that he did not join the search for his missing neighbour, or go to her wake, further damaged his credibility in the eyes of the jury. Above all, David O'Shea's incoherent and misleading account of his movements on the evening of 8 February confirmed his guilt. His answers showed he had no alibi for the time of the murder, and was trying to conceal this fact.

The judge's summing up did nothing to help the defence case, since it began with a dissertation on necrophilia, which reminded the jury how vicious the murder had been. He then considered the question of premeditation, an important question in deciding whether the accused should hang if he was found guilty. The judge's comments on Civic Guard Keane's testimony suggested he believed he was telling the truth. He said that if the policeman had invented the conversation he was 'a devil out of hell', and he did not think a civic guard would do such a thing. He then stated that the dialogue was so natural that if it was made up the witness had great ability as a playwright. It must be said that even if Keane's testimony were discounted, the remaining evidence damned David O'Shea as the murderer of Ellen O'Sullivan. The jury returned a verdict of guilty, although they added the rider that the murder was not premeditated, and was committed during a period of abnormality. The judge passed the mandatory death sentence, but promised their comments would be passed on to the proper authorities for consideration. The plea that this statement amounted to a guilty but insane verdict was later rejected by the Appeals Court, and David O'Shea was hanged six months later.

THE DRUMCONDRA CHANCER

The Dublin slang word 'chancer' is applied to the sort of conman who will lie or make up an outrageous story at the drop of a hat. The used car dealer who tries to sell you a twelve-year-old Lada or Yugo automobile at twice its market price because 'Sure, and aren't they going to be collector's cars in a few years', could be described as a chancer. So might the politician who declares that once in power his party will simultaneously lower taxes and double social welfare payments. John Fleming's tales, told in the pursuit of love (or at least sex) eventually brought him to the gallows. His crime was a clumsy, desperate act, and so badly executed a donkey could have solved it. Yet this third-rate murderer showed that, in the hunt for romance, his barefaced nerve was unequalled. Few men have lied so consistently or so well, when trapped between two women, and for that Fleming ranks with the greatest chancers in the annals of Irish crime.

In the early evening of 26 July 1933, the nephew and sister of Mrs Ellen Fleming arrived at a railway station in Dublin expecting to find her waiting for them. She was not there, so they went to her home in Drumcondra, which they found locked and apparently empty. The nephew, who lodged with Mrs Fleming, collected a spare key from a neighbour and they entered the small terraced house. They found the woman they were seeking lying dead on the parlour floor, dressed and ready to go out. Somebody had battered her head repeatedly with a heavy object. The Gardai later discovered that this weapon was a claw hammer, probably one that had gone missing from the house. They estimated the murder happened around 5 p.m., about three hours before the body was discovered.

Mrs Fleming's husband John could not be found at first, but was traced a few hours later to a friend's house. He was remarkably calm when asked to accompany the Gardai to the police station to be questioned about a murder, and did not even bother to ask who the victim was. Under interrogation, he suggested the murderer of Mrs Fleming might be an insurance salesman who was due to call that afternoon, but the accusations of the Gardai were pointed directly at him. Forensic tests revealed that John Fleming's clothes were spattered with minute traces of human blood, and he was also the last person who admitted to seeing her alive. Police inquiries into the husband's shocking extra-marital activities confirmed their suspicions, as did further information they received about an earlier murder attempt on Mrs Fleming. John Fleming was arrested shortly after the murder, and remanded in custody to await trial for killing his wife.

The train of events whose climax was the battering to death of Ellen Fleming began harmlessly enough about five years previously. Her husband, enjoying his daily lunch at the Central Café in Dublin's D'Olier Street, began chatting to his waitress, an attractive sixteen-year-old girl named Rita Murtagh. John Fleming, a draper, was originally from the west of Ireland, and had travelled in his youth before settling down and marrying Ellen, who was about fifteen years older and comparatively well off. He was in his early thirties when he met the pretty waitress from the working class suburb of Stoneybatter. She was impressed by his good looks and impeccable manners, while he found her youth and innocence irresistible. Over the following months, Cupid's arrows began to fly between the couple. After about a year of exchanging lingering glances over his meat and two veg, Fleming and Miss Murtagh began to go out together. He neglected to mention that he was married, and told her he lived with a maiden aunt. Gradually, as the relationship with Miss Murtagh deepened into love, the question arose of the couple becoming engaged. Fleming said that, much as he wished to tie the knot with his girlfriend, there was a problem. He had made a financial agreement with his 'aunt', and could not afford to move out for the present. He brought Rita Murtagh back to see the house in Drumcondra when his wife was out. The girl, he explained to Mrs Fleming's nephew, was a niece from the country whom he had promised to keep an eye out for.

Rita Murtagh was a respectable working-class Catholic girl, and believed that it was a sin to have sex with a man before marriage. These views did not sit well with her boyfriend, but she held him at bay for a very long time. They had been courting for almost four years when she finally succumbed to the draper's charms, after accompanying him home one night. Ellen Fleming was away for a few days visiting relatives, and her husband had no qualms about borrowing the marital bed for the seduction. The couple now began making love at every opportunity, and their nights of passion in the 'aunt's' house became a regular occurrence whenever she was away. Rita Murtagh got the permission of her parents – who were either extremely naive or knew a good catch for their daughter when they saw one – to stay out overnight with her boyfriend.

If the Murtagh family were expecting their daughter to become engaged in the near future, they were in for a severe disappointment. John Fleming, once the couple had entered into a sexual relationship, became less interested in his girlfriend's wedding plans. Rita Murtagh was now entirely committed to her handsome draper, and was desperate to hear the sound of wedding bells. She hinted that the irregular situation could not continue indefinitely without ruining her reputation. John Fleming placated her with vague promises, but began to realize that he could not fob off his lover indefinitely.

The strain of meeting the conflicting expectations of two demanding women would drive any man to distraction, even an accomplished liar like John Fleming. On 31 March 1932 he made a determined effort to resolve his quandary by murdering his wife. That evening, her nephew knocked on the door of the next-door neighbour, Mrs O'Rourke. He begged her to come and help his aunt, who had suddenly been taken ill. The woman found Mrs Fleming writhing in agony and moaning that her husband had poisoned her. John Fleming, who was in the room, ignored these accusations. He went out to look for a doctor to treat his wife, but came back alone thirty minutes later. Mrs O'Rourke ran next door and woke up her brother-in-law, who was a trained army nurse. He examined the sick woman, and told her husband he must find a doctor immediately. Fleming hurried off and was gone for nearly an hour. Once again, he did not return with any medical help, and excused himself by saying he could not get an answer at the doctor's house. Mrs Fleming now asked for a drink, which her husband offered to make for her. After one mouthful she pushed the glass away, and complained that it was 'bitter like the chocolates you gave me'. Mrs O'Rourke demanded that John Fleming let her have the glass, but as she reached out for it the patient had another spasm. Fleming 'accidentally' spilt the contents, and again hurried off on the pretext of going to find a doctor. Twenty minutes later, he returned with a glass of whiskey for Mrs Fleming, but she flatly refused to touch it.

The army nurse thought that Mrs Fleming was suffering from the effects of strychnine poisoning. He did not directly accuse her husband, but noted his erratic behaviour and reluctance to find a doctor for his wife. At about 4 a.m., Mrs O'Rourke remembered there was a nurse living nearby. This woman, a Nurse MacDonagh, was summoned and took over the care of the sick woman. Before he went back to bed, Mrs O'Rourke's brother-in-law warned the nurse that he believed Mrs Fleming had been poisoned. He asked her to inform the doctor of his suspicions, since he was due to leave the next morning, and would be unable to notify the Gardai himself. The doctor, when he finally arrived on the following afternoon, found Mrs Fleming much better. After talking with her husband, he decided she was not seriously ill, and prescribed a tonic for her nerves. The draper told him that he had only pretended to look for a doctor earlier, since he knew there was nothing wrong with Ellen. Incredibly Fleming escaped being apprehended on this occasion, and the authorities only became interested in the causes of his wife's sickness much later. Then they found out that the draper had obtained some strychnine shortly before the incident, on the pretext of wishing to kill a dangerous dog.

Fleming's failed murder attempt released him – at least for the time being – from the web of lies in which had entangled himself. Ellen Fleming was terrified after her ordeal, and fled to her relatives in the country. For the first time, John

Fleming was free to throw himself into his affair with Rita Murtagh without worrying about his wife. Things went well, and for months he was able to enjoy the pleasures of marriage without any of its responsibilities. This ideal situation was brought to an end in February 1933, when his girlfriend tearfully informed him she was pregnant. The couple, if they wished to avoid the anger of her father, would have to be married within the very near future. Another man might have been fazed by the fact that he already had a wife, but not the irrepressible John Fleming. He said they would marry in the following August, and a few days later the couple purchased engagement and wedding rings at a well-known Dublin jewellers. Rita was delighted, even though Fleming did not pay for the rings because they had to be left in for alteration. She could not know her future 'husband' had no intention of collecting them, and gave a false name on the receipt. With grim humour, Fleming called himself Mr Lemming. His choice of alias was appropriate, for like the Arctic rodent he was racing towards a precipice from which he could not draw back.

Rita Murtagh, unaware of her lover's duplicity, announced her impending marriage to her friends and family. Fleming, meanwhile, found himself forced to deal with an unexpected crisis. In April 1933, Ellen Fleming came back from the country. She informed her husband that she had forgiven him and wished to re-establish marital relations. Considering that he had dosed her with one of the most agonizing poisons known to man, it was a remarkably generous gesture. This did not help John Fleming, who was unable to stop her moving back into the house. He was forced to resume his exhausting double life, and once again had to appease both his unwanted wife and worried fiancée. To make matters worse, people were beginning to gossip about his adulterous behaviour. Dublin is a small city, and it was inevitable that sooner or later somebody would realize that Ellen Fleming's husband and Rita Murtagh's boyfriend were one and the same man. Eventually the rumours reached the ears of the younger woman, and John Fleming was faced with a dilemma that could only be resolved by murder.

Rita Murtagh, by now six months pregnant, confronted her boyfriend in June 1933. She repeated the gossip she had heard and demanded to know if he already had a wife. He immediately denied the accusation, saying it was a malicious lie being circulated by his enemies. Somebody was deliberately confusing him with another John Fleming, who happened to live further along the same road as his aunt. He offered to bring her along to meet the man, so she would know he was telling her the truth. This pacified Rita for the moment, but her father was not quite as gullible.

On 21 July 1933, he insisted on speaking with Fleming alone, and warned him to prove once and for all that he was a single man; otherwise he could expect to face some unpleasant consequences. Fleming won some time by arranging to bring proof of his unmarried status within a week, but he was at the end of his tether. The liar who could have bluffed his way into Heaven had run out of lies. Within five days, Fleming had decided on a course of action, and the wife he hated lay dead.

The week-long trial of John Fleming began on 14 November 1933. Rita Murtagh had, by now, had her baby and so was spared from having to face the packed courtroom whilst still heavy with the accused man's child. She was not spared much else. Those who heard her pathetic tale of seduction and betrayal did not know whether to laugh or to cry. The ordeal was so upsetting that she fainted twice on the witness stand, and had to be carried from the courtroom for medical treatment. Eventually the judge in the case showed some sympathy for her predicament, and gave her permission to testify in a chair with its back to the crowded gallery. Her intimate account of the relationship with Fleming was corroborated by her parents' evidence. The revelations in court about his previous attempt to kill Ellen Fleming sealed the fate of the man in the dock.

Fleming, when he took the stand to refute the allegations that he was a seducer and murderer, did what he was best at. He lied. He stated that he was completely innocent, and had nothing to do with the death of his wife. If there was blood on his clothes, it was because of a cut on his finger. He never gave Ellen poison, he loved his wife and would not hurt her. But when he thought of it there had been some crumbs of strychnine in the pocket of his jacket. These might have tainted the chocolates he brought home that day, although he did not remember her eating any of them. Fleming then demolished any illusions that Rita Murtagh might have still had about his opinion of her. When asked whether he ever intended to marry his mistress, he simply replied 'No.' He offered his view of the relationship:

Question: Had you any genuine feeling for her?
Fleming: I rather liked the girl, her manner and ways. I had no particular reason.
Question: For what?
Fleming: I suppose it is a case of the weakness of human nature; the friendship grew between us.

Question: I am asking if you had any genuine affection for
the girl? Don't mind about the human nature.

Fleming: No, I had not.

At the end of the trial, the jury took less than two hours
to find the draper guilty, and the judge issued the death
sentence. Fleming reacted by demanding an appeal on the
grounds that he was an innocent man. A petition for clemency was refused and the date of the hanging was set for 5
January 1934. On that day, John Fleming – draper, ruthless
seducer and incomparable liar – went to the gallows still
proclaiming he did not murder his wife. His executioner
was Thomas Pierrepoint, the noted British hangman. In the
course of his long career, he presided over four hundred
executions, including some of the most famous criminals
of the twentieth century. Thomas Pierrepoint, like his more
famous nephew Albert, was often hired to carry out hang-
ings in the Irish Republic, which had no resident hangman.
Pierrepoint was famed for his efficiency and speed as a
hangman; he so was skilful that he could execute a man
within the twelve strokes of a noonday clock. It was poetic
justice that Fleming, the prince of chancers, should meet
his death at the hands of the prince of hangmen.

WAS SHE MAD?

In 1912, the marriage took place of Fanny Malone, a petite spinster from Londonderry, in her mid-thirties, and William Barber, a sergeant in the Royal Irish Constabulary, based in Belfast at the RIC's city headquarters. He was fifty-six, a widower, with two grown children; and a niece, Isabel Martin, had been his housekeeper since his wife's death in 1907. After his second marriage, Isabel Martin continued in this position. Despite his failure to rise beyond the rank of sergeant, Barber had always been careful with his money and had a tidy sum in the bank. On his retirement from the RIC in 1921, he sold his house in Belfast and bought two adjacent houses in Cultra, a pleasant dormitory and resort village, between Holywood and Bangor, overlooking Belfast Lough.

Mr and Mrs Barber, with Isabel Martin still as house-keeper, occupied the larger of the two houses, and two rooms were let to lodgers. The other house was demolished and a bungalow built on the site, rented by the Barbers to a Peter Conlon. Despite his RIC pension and the rentals he was receiving, Barber took a new job. This was as a rent collector for the Belfast property company, A. & J. Turner. The Turner properties were slum buildings and the job of rent collector was a risky one, more from the potential violence of the tenants than from any fear of robbery on the street. William Barber still had his police revolver and carried that when he went out on his work. At other times, he kept it on top of his bedroom wardrobe.

By late 1933, Barber was an elderly man – seventy-eight years old, but he was fit and well, and still carrying out his rent-collecting duties. He was a tall, broad figure, well over six feet, dwarfing his wife, Fanny, who at four foot two scarcely reached his shoulder. They had by now been married for twenty-one years. On Christmas Eve of that year, Peter Conlon, in his flimsily built bungalow right beside the Barbers' house, heard two odd noises, separated by about twenty minutes. One had sounded like a picture dropping from a wall, the other like a car door being slammed. He thought nothing of this until he heard a frantic knocking at his back door. Fanny Barber and Isabel Martin were both there, in a state of high agitation. Fanny asked him to come over to her house. 'Something's happened,' she said. Isabel added her plea to come quickly, adding, rather strangely, 'Auntie's in terrible trouble.'

Conlon wanted to know more, and Fanny asked him if he had seen or heard a prowler at the back of her house. Conlon had seen nothing at all, but admitted to having heard a couple of unusual noises. Mrs Barber seized on this, and said a man had been hiding in her garden all evening. Isabel told Conlon that she had been out, and had found on coming back that Fanny had locked herself inside the house.

Conlon accompanied the two distraught women as they led him towards the back door of the house, which was reached through the garage. 'Why don't we go in the front door?' he asked. 'My darling's lying in the hall,' was Fanny's answer. As they went in, the Barbers' two dogs rushed up, barking, as they always did when anyone approached the house. They went through the house to the front hall, where Conlon was horrified to see William Barber slumped against the bolted front door. He was in a seated position, and he had gunshot wounds under his right ear and in the chest. His left forearm was across his lap and balanced on it was a gun. Isabel Martin screamed and Conlon caught her as she fell in a faint.

'Mr Conlon, who could have done that to my poor darling?' cried Fanny.

They went back to the bungalow, from where Conlon rang for the police. He then went back for a second look at Barber, and confirmed that the old man was indeed dead, but that his hands were not yet cold. Soon after that, a sergeant and two constables arrived, followed by a doctor. Dr Donnan confirmed that William Barber had been shot twice. The shot below the ear had been fired at very close range, leaving the ear itself blackened with powder; the other appeared to have been fired from a greater distance. It seemed that both bullets had entered the body on a downwards trajectory. The gun itself, the presumed murder – or was it suicide? – weapon, was a five-chambered revolver. Two bullets remained unfired. But what had happened to the third bullet? There was no sign of it anywhere. The police officers then examined the kitchen, where they found a fresh scar gouged in the middle bar of a chair.

The senior police officer, Sergeant Patton, searched the body and found that the dead man still had his gold watch and chain, and the substantial sum for those days of £46 in coins and banknotes, plus some loose change. Clearly robbery was not a motive.

The key witness was obviously the newly widowed Fanny Barber. Although she was still distraught, Patton was able to take a statement from her. The day had been a normal one until after 8 p.m. The two Barbers, Isabel, and Mrs Dornan, their only lodger at the time, had eaten supper together. Mrs Dornan then left to catch a bus, as she was spending Christmas with her family in Dundonald. William Barber volunteered to escort her to the bus-stop, but Fanny would not allow it, as he was newly recovered from a cold, so Isabel Martin went with her. This was around 8.30 p.m. Fanny then described how, as she and her husband were sitting in the kitchen, a man came rushing in through the back door. He made for Fanny as if to grab her, but she jumped up and escaped upstairs, where she locked herself in her bedroom. The man was in his forties, she thought, with a red moustache, and wearing a dirty grey suit. His cap was pulled down as though to help hide his face, and he had a brown scarf round his neck. One hand was thrust into his pocket, as though holding a hidden weapon. Fanny heard the sounds of a struggle below, then two shots. On that, she said, she had fainted, and only came to again when Isabel was ringing at the front doorbell. Sergeant Patton then produced the gun which had been placed on the body, and asked Mrs Barber if she could identify it as her husband's. After some hesitation, Fanny agreed that it was. She also confirmed it was normally kept on top of the bedroom wardrobe.

Following the sergeant's report, two police inspectors came to the house on Christmas Day. They found the third bullet under a couch in the kitchen, and concluded that it had been fired at Barber as he sat in the chair, and had ricocheted from the chair to the wall and thence to the floor. On Boxing Day, Fanny Barber's doctor was called to the house. He pronounced Fanny to be insane, and she was taken to the Mental Hospital at Downpatrick, where she remained for five months.

The inconsistencies of Fanny's story had not been lost on the police. When the inquest on William Barber was held, accidental death or suicide were both ruled out. The verdict was murder by a person unknown. The police were, however, in little doubt. After Fanny's release from the hospital in Downpatrick, they arrested her on the 27th of September 1934, and charged her with the murder of her husband. Despite the protests of her solicitor, and her own screams, she was remanded to Armagh Prison. Eight days later, at a special court convened in Holywood, a preliminary hearing opened. Fanny pleaded not guilty. Although her story was dubious at best, the prosecution still had a difficult task. Prosecuting counsel was Richard Carson, KC. Of the three essentials for the committing of a serious crime, motive, weapon and opportunity, the latter two had clearly been present. Fanny and William had been alone in the house – assuming the tale about the intruder was a fabrication – and the gun was available. Carson's aim was to establish motive. He elicited from Conlon that not long before, in response to a casual remark about her husband's continuing good health, Fanny had responded, 'I wonder if the old fool will ever die.'

It was not much, but it was something. During his cross-examination of Isabel Martin, a confused and hesitant witness, he was able to establish that Isabel knew of insurance policies taken out by Fanny on her husband's life, and that Barber had been unaware of these. Again, there was nothing illegal or necessarily underhand about this – many wives did this, knowing that their husbands would not agree, and knowing also that they might otherwise be ill-provided for as widows. Fanny's doctor also helped, probably unintentionally, by saying that she had told him she thought her neighbours believed her to be insane. Gradually, the prosecution was building up a case that might impress the magistrates, and in due course a jury, particularly when added to the circumstances of the fatal evening. Fanny was duly remanded for trial.

Somewhat oddly, the trial was fixed for the 1935 Winter Assizes in Londonderry, Fanny's home town, and a long way from Cultra. Her Derry connections inevitably made it a high-profile event in the city. Prosecuting counsel was A.B. Babington, later to be a lord chief justice of Northern Ireland. He began by exposing the inconsistent story of the intruder. When Isabel had rung at the front door, why should Fanny have called to her, from upstairs, to go in by the back door? After all, Fanny was not supposed to have known her husband's body was blocking the front door. Babington also queried why Fanny did not call for help. Her upstairs window overlooked the street. And he raised the matter of the dogs – why had they not been heard barking if there was a man lurking about the house? There was no sign of a struggle, no robbery, no trace of the man with the red moustache had ever been found. He was, Babington concluded, an invention of Fanny Barber's, to cloak her own guilt. It was a strong case.

Fanny's counsel, William Lowry, KC, concentrated on the vital matter of proof. However damning were the circumstances, the prosecution would have to prove beyond all reasonable doubt that Fanny had fired the shots. The police, as Sergeant Patton had to admit, had failed to find her fingerprints, or anyone else's, on the revolver. One of Patton's colleagues, Constable Kieren, added to the circumstantial evidence by testifying to a conversation he had had with Fanny on the night of the murder. She had complained about Barber's meanness. 'He was an old scrounge. He never gave me anything, only what barely kept the house.' And more significantly, 'He made a will in favour of me, if I can prove there is nothing wrong with me.' For if Fanny Barber were certified insane, she would be legally unable to inherit. And yet, ironically, insanity might save her from the gallows.

Barber's will had indeed left everything to Fanny. The life insurance policies totalled a modest £272 – hardly a sum to kill for. Her counsel defended the reality of the intruder, suggesting he could have followed the rent collector back from Belfast; and that he might have wrested the gun from Barber. Babington had pointed out, among other inconsistencies in Fanny's account, that she would appear to have fainted for a most unusual length of time, more than half an hour. The summing-up by Mr Justice Brown leant slightly in favour of the accused, but the jury failed to reach a verdict. There would have to be a retrial.

This took place at Downpatrick in the spring of 1935 before Lord Justice Andrews, and with the same counsel. There was no new evidence, and it was a straight test of the two barristers' ability to marshal the facts as they stood, for or against the defendant. The plea remained not guilty. If the possibility of an admission of guilt, linked to a plea of unsound mind, were considered, it was only to be rejected. Fanny would be free but penniless, and liable to be confined in an asylum. Babington set out to batter the statements given by Fanny and to reduce her credibility to zero. Why had she said nothing to Isabel Martin about the intruder? Why did her story to Conlon differ from that she later gave to the police? Why had she failed to raise the alarm? Fanny could only fall back on saying she could not remember making these statements, even one which she had signed. Lowry again dwelt on the lack of any definite forensic evidence linking Fanny with the shooting, and also on the great difference in height between her and her husband. How could such a small woman have fired shots that entered his body downwards? There was high tension as the jury returned from their deliberation. But even before the word 'Guilty' was uttered, Fanny Barber, sensing what was to come, screamed and fainted. Isabel Martin also showed great emotion and was led in hysterics from the courtroom. When Fanny was revived, and through her continued barrage of screams, the judge sentenced her to be hanged by the neck until dead, for the murder of William Barber.

In the end, the sentence was commuted to one of life imprisonment, and Fanny Barber eventually died in gaol in 1952. One of the intriguing aspects of the case is the role of Isabel Martin, who throughout appears to have supported Fanny rather than her murdered uncle. No doubt Isabel, like Fanny, had suffered from the old man's meanness. Isabel's remark to Peter Conlon ('Auntie's in terrible trouble'), her reluctance to even look at what might have happened to Barber, and her emotion when Fanny was sentenced, seem strange but any conclusions concerning these aspects must remain speculative.

THE QUARE FELLA

It is a curious fact that two of Ireland's most famous writers were inspired to write masterpieces after witnessing executions whilst in prison. This may tell us something about the dangers of pursuing a literary life but it says more about the traumatic nature of capital punishment. Oscar Wilde's 'The Ballad of Reading Gaol', based on the execution in 1897 of Trooper Charles Wooldridge for the stabbing of his wife, concerns an English murder. The protagonist of the second of these literary works, on the other hand, was an Irishman. His name was Bernard Kirwan, but he will be remembered by the name that Brendan Behan gave him in the play first staged at the Pike Theatre, Dublin, in 1954 – The Quare Fella.

The manhunt that brought Bernard Kirwan to the gallows started with a chance conversation between a vigilant Garda and the brother of a labourer who worked on the Kirwan farm in County Offaly. The man mentioned that Lar Kirwan, one of the two brothers who lived there, had gone off on holiday to see his aunt in Kildare. The policeman, who knew that Lar was at daggers drawn with his sibling Bernard, decided he should check this information out. He spoke to Peter Kirwan, an elder brother of both, who had left home to open a butcher's shop in a nearby village. This brother was surprised to hear Lar had gone away, so the Garda contacted his superiors. They called on the aunt and found the missing brother was not there. His girlfriend was also wondering where he could have gone to. The couple had arranged to meet in Tullamore on the previous Saturday evening, but Lar never arrived; she was still waiting to hear from him. The Gardai launched a search for the missing man, and soon came to believe his brother Bernard had murdered him.

The motives behind the suspected homicide were two of the oldest known to mankind – sibling rivalry and a disputed inheritance. The animosity between Lar and Bernard Kirwan had its seeds in 1903, when their father, a retired RIC constable from Galway, bought a small cottage and forty acres at Ballincloghan, a few miles outside of Tullamore, County Offaly. Kirwan senior died in 1912, and his widow Mary did not remarry, preferring to raise their six children on her own. As they grew to adulthood, the children left to be married or to work elsewhere, until by 1936 only the mother and her sons Bernard and Lawrence remained on the farm. The characters of the two men were very different – Bernard, the elder of the two, being generous, lazy and a heavy drinker, whilst Lar was mean, industrious and sober.

In 1936, inspired perhaps by the Western movies he saw in the picture house in Tullamore, the reckless Bernard committed an armed robbery. He sawed the barrels off his shotgun, and waylaid a postman cycling between the scattered farmhouses with registered mail. He stole the man's postal bag and shot off the bicycle's tyre, then fled away across the fields. He did not get away with the theft, since he was recognized by the postman and arrested within hours. Bernard Kirwan was sentenced to seven years' imprisonment. He served his time in Portlaoise Prison, where he worked as a pork butcher in the gaol's slaughterhouse. A year into his sentence, he received news that his mother was dead. Mary Kirwan, no doubt wishing to avoid dissension in the family, willed that the farm be sold and its proceeds divided equally between her six children. Unfortunately the mortgage and other debts on the farm exceeded its total value. Because of these circumstances, the brothers and sisters, with the exception of Bernard, agreed Lar should keep the farm and continue running it by himself.

In 1941, the authorities released Bernard Kirwan from prison on licence. He returned to Ballincloghan only to find himself an unwanted interloper in his own home. Lar had replaced him with a farm labourer named Jack Foran, and made it very clear he now considered he owned the farm. At first, he would not even let Bernard into the cottage, and the released convict was forced to take shelter with his married sister. A week or so later, Lar grudgingly allowed Bernard to move in, on condition he helped work the farm, but he refused to pay him a proper wage. Bernard then retaliated by stealing £15 from his brother, and going on a binge in Dublin to celebrate his release from prison. When he got back to Ballincloghan, his quarrel with the enraged Lar, who was determined to starve his feckless brother out of the farm, escalated into an open feud.

The petty warfare between the Kirwan brothers would have been farcical, were it not for the tragic denouement to the story. First Lar locked the food cupboard, so Bernard could eat nothing beyond the meagre dinner he was given. The older brother stopped helping with the farm work, and defied his sibling to do something about it. A few weeks later, their relations further deteriorated when Lar realized food was disappearing from his locked store. In retaliation, he bought himself a second-hand car, whilst still telling Bernard he had no money to give him from their shared inheritance. One night in August, the ex-convict came home roaring drunk, to find Lar had locked him out of the cottage.

He immediately smashed the lock and staggered off to his bed. The next morning, when Lar discovered the broken front door, he shook his brother awake and began cursing him. They started to fight, and Jack Foran rushed in to find Lar had been knifed in the hand.

Bernard, feeling unrepentant about the incident, boasted he would stab Lar to death the next time they fought. Food was still mysteriously disappearing from the store cupboard, so Lar now moved the supplies to the locked boot of his old car. He thought he had trumped his older brother, but a few days later found a bar of soap with the imprint of his car key pressed into it. Bernard was planning to copy the key so he could help himself to the food in the boot. Lar changed the lock and began sleeping with the keys in his pocket. By now, the atmosphere between the brothers was poisonous, and the feud had become the talk of the area. Both men had their supporters: Bernard's said that his younger brother had no right to deny him a share in the family farm; Lar's replied he worked hard for what he earned, and shouldn't have to throw it away on a drunkard and wastrel. The bad feelings in the tiny cottage continued unabated through the long, warm summer and the mellow autumn. By the beginning of winter it seemed inevitable that the dispute between the brothers must soon reach its violent conclusion.

On Thursday 20 November 1941, Lar Kirwan and the labourer, Jack Foran, drove four cattle off to market in Tullamore, staying overnight at a friend's farm so they would arrive early the following morning. Lar sold four cattle for £50, the second such sale made by him in a few weeks. Afterwards he bought a sack of flour from a local merchant, leaving behind a five-shilling deposit, which would be refunded when he returned the empty sack.

When they arrived back at the cottage in Ballincloghan, Lar ordered Jack Foran to clean out the boiler room, which hadn't been used for nearly a year. To the labourer's surprise the filthy job had already been done; there was even an unlit fire waiting in its grate. The only person who could have performed this unpleasant task was Bernard, who hadn't lifted a finger around the farm for weeks.

The following day was a Saturday. Lar worked around the farm, and tried to fix his bicycle. Foran helped him pour the flour into the store, after which Lar placed the bag on the carrier of his bike to bring it into Tullamore that evening. During the afternoon, Bernard asked the labourer to do some errands in the town. He paid for them with coins from a bulging pouch, which looked like the one Lar kept his savings in. In the early evening, the labourer rode off to Tullamore on Bernard's bike, leaving his employer working in the yard. Around 8 p.m. his neighbours observed Lar as he drove his cows home from the fields. Afterwards he planned to go into Tullamore to meet a friend and his fiancée, as was his usual habit on a Saturday night.

The last person to have seen Lar Kirwan was his brother, who said the missing man was still in the house at 9 p.m., when he himself went out. If Bernard went out at all, he was back by midnight, at which time Jack Foran returned to find him in the kitchen. He was wearing Lar's wellington boots and dungarees. Bernard was unusually friendly with the farm labourer, and made him a mug of cocoa before going to bed. Foran slept late on Sunday morning, but when he arose Bernard gave him the day off. In the afternoon, smoke was observed pouring from the boiler house by an old couple on a neighbouring farm. On the next day, a Monday, Bernard sent Foran to cut reeds for thatching in a marsh some miles away. The young man did not get back to the cottage until evening, when he learnt his new employer had neglected to do any of the daily farm chores. Bernard excused his negligence by explaining he had spent the day clearing rubbish out of the cottage and sheds. During the course of the day his neighbours once again saw copious clouds of black smoke coming from the boiler house.

Over the next few days, Foran realized that Bernard Kirwan was not expecting Lar to be coming home in the near future. From the older brother's actions, it was obvious he had assumed control of the farm, and was now in charge of its finances. During the week, Bernard went into Tullamore and paid some outstanding rates on the property. Afterwards he visited a local tailor to buy himself a new suit.

If Bernard really thought he could fend off speculation about Lar Kirwan's sudden disappearance with vague tales about a holiday, he was living in a fantasy world. It was not long until the Gardai came knocking on the cottage door to inquire about his brother's whereabouts. The police arranged to have a missing persons appeal broadcast on the national radio service, but in private they speculated that Lar was already dead, and his remains buried in some remote field or bog.

George Lawlor of the Garda Technical Unit came down from Dublin to assist with the inquiry, and large-scale searches of the Ballincloghan area were undertaken. Nothing came to light, and as the months passed by, it seemed increasingly unlikely that Lar Kirwan's body would ever be found.

The detectives assigned to the case concentrated on finding evidence supporting their theory that Bernard had killed his brother on the Saturday night. A search of the cottage on

16 December 1941 uncovered Lar's watch, empty money pouch and his tobacco pipe. These personal items, which he would not have left at home if he were going out, were locked in a drawer. Interviews with his friends and acquaintances confirmed he was not seen in Tullamore on the night of 22 November, nor on the road into the town from Ballincloghan. During a further search on Christmas Eve, the Gardai found a burnt fragment of one of his pullovers. All of these clues indicated Lar Kirwan had not left the house alive on that night in November.

The police received a lucky break when Bernard was arrested for burglary, and had to pay his solicitor £70 to represent him. Forensic experts examined the notes, and found they were marked by traces of the lining of Lar's money pouch. Bernard had earlier claimed to be almost penniless, but detectives calculated his expenditure in recent weeks at almost a hundred pounds. This matched Lar Kirwan's profit from the sale of the two lots of cattle at Tullamore market. Bernard was placed under surveillance, and in March 1942 an officer observed he was wearing an unfamiliar black overcoat. On approaching the suspect, he observed the garment was dyed, and confiscated it for examination. The missing man's girlfriend, a dressmaker by profession, recognized the garment as Lar Kirwan's brown coat, and pointed out a repair she had made on the sleeve. Bernard insisted he had purchased the overcoat at the Tullamore market. None of the traders recognized the garment, but a shopkeeper in the town stated the suspect had recently bought three packets of black dye. In April 1942, Lar Kirwan's bike was discovered on a first cousin's farm, where it had been hidden in a derelict hay shed. The flour sack on its carrier was missing, but later turned up in the attic of the cottage. It seemed likely that Bernard had concealed it there, planning to reclaim the five-shilling deposit at a later date.

George Lawlor and his colleagues had amassed a strong circumstantial case against their principal suspect. Nevertheless it was unlikely they would be able to charge him with murder unless they found Lar's body. Murderers are sometimes convicted without the victim's body being recovered, but it is fairly unusual and makes a case much more difficult to prove. In 1936, for example, a young man in Dublin named Edward Ball was convicted for murdering his mother, even though he threw her body in the Irish Sea and it could not be reclaimed. But in that case there was tangible evidence that a crime had taken place, in the form of bloodstains in the missing woman's car. Although Lar Kirwan had disappeared, and the Gardai were certain his brother Bernard was guilty of murder, there were no forensic clues to show that an act of violence had taken place. Without these, all the Gardai could do was wait and hope that Lar's body would eventually be discovered. Bernard, who was out on bail after a short spell in custody, continued working the farm, whilst bitterly complaining the police were persecuting him.

The stalemate between the Gardai and their suspect ended on 29 May 1942. On that day, two farmers, clearing a drainage trench at turf cuttings in Ballinacor Bog, found a sack containing human remains. On close examination, they were discovered to be the trunk of a male aged between twenty and fifty years. The body part was between six and eighteen months old, and had been skillfully dismembered by somebody with surgical or veterinary skills – such as those acquired by Bernard Kirwan when he worked as a butcher in Portlaoise Prison. The sack was identified as being of the same make as one missing from the cottage, in which Lar Kirwan had kept his tools. (Jack Foran had stated that this sack was draped over the handle of the binding machine in the yard, but all the Gardai could find were the scattered tools.)

Bernard Kirwan was arrested in August 1942, and stood trial in January of the following year. There was no way of determining the victim's cause of death, but the evidence that he had been murdered by his brother was irrefutable. Bernard Kirwan further damaged his own defence whilst in prison, by attempting to smuggle out a letter requesting a friend to provide a false alibi for the Saturday night. The prosecution based its case on seven separate points, and nearly one hundred witnesses were called to support the allegations. Bernard faced his inescapable conviction with the familiar mixture of bluff and arrogance he displayed throughout the inquiry. When asked why he should not be sentenced to death he replied 'At the outset of this case I pleaded not guilty. Throughout this trial I have reiterated my innocence, and that is all I have to say. For all the sins of my life I ask forgiveness of God and no forgiveness of man.' His final comment as he was being led from the court was 'I forgive my enemies.' Bernard Kirwan, the 'Quare Fella', was hanged in Mountjoy Prison for his fratricidal murder on 2 June 1943.

THE CROSSMOLINA
PAEDOPHILE

The fear that their child might be abducted and murdered is one that most modern parents have experienced. This was not always so. Fifty years ago, our society was not so obsessed with the need to protect its younger members from the attention of predatory adults. Children in rural Ireland were free to come and go as they pleased, with little concern for their safety. Then a ghastly murder in Mayo shattered the illusion that their innocence was sacrosanct. Many Irish people, for the first time in their lives, were forced to acknowledge the dark sexual impulses that lurk in the psyche of some human beings.

On a bright Sunday morning in June 1945, eight and a half-year-old Michael Loftus went off to play in the fields around the family farm at Crossmolina, County Mayo. By evening he had not returned, and his parents began to be concerned for his safety. The next morning saw a full search of the Crossmolina area inaugurated, and for days a mixed party of Gardai and local people scoured the surrounding countryside. One week later, Michael's father found a patch of newly dug earth under a gorse bush in a remote field. When the Gardai investigated the spot, it proved to be a shallow grave about two feet deep containing the body of the missing child. Somebody had beaten his head in with an unknown implement.

A search of the vicinity revealed a pair of boots,

half-hidden in a hedgerow about a third of a mile from the grave. The Gardai, suspecting these might point to the murderer, did not remove them. Instead two officers concealed themselves nearby, in order to see if anybody returned to collect them. Their efforts were rewarded that evening, when they noticed a shadowy figure creeping up the field towards the place where the boots were hidden. The officers leapt out and apprehended a thirty-year-old neighbour of the Loftus family called Stephen Murphy, who told them he was looking for a lost cow. The Gardai accepted this information and released him, but made a note to keep him under observation. The next evening, he was again stopped by Gardai, who saw him behaving suspiciously in the vicinity of a nearby ring fort. This time he attempted to run away, but when caught admitted he had just left an old pair of trousers in the fort. They were retrieved and taken away for forensic inspection.

Murphy, by now the Gardai's chief suspect in the murder of Michael Loftus, was interviewed on several occasions. He claimed to have found the trousers, which had a number of suspicious stains, in a deserted house. He could give no coherent explanation of his reasons for hiding them in the fort. When asked about Michael Loftus, he replied that he did not know the boy well, although the Gardai soon discovered that they had been almost inseparable for months. Stephen Murphy kept ferrets, and would often take Michael with him to hunt rabbits in the woods. On the day before the murder, Murphy was seen cycling along with the boy perched on his crossbar. The autopsy report indicated the source of Murphy's interest in his much younger friend, and provided him with a strong motive for killing the little boy.

The blows of a spade had fatally crushed the skull of

Michael Loftus, leaving huge gashes on his head and face. The condition of the boy's anus, moreover, indicated that he had been subjected to sustained sexual abuse over a long period of time. The Gardai knew immediately that the person who inflicted this treatment was also his murderer – the child had been killed to stop him telling his parents or friends what had been done to him. All the evidence pointed to Stephen Murphy as both the abuser and murderer of Michael Loftus, and he was taken into custody. At first, the suspect refuted all the accusations of the Gardai, but after several days of interrogation he changed his mind and made a full confession of his guilt. The Gardai, intent on obtaining evidence that would confirm his statement, asked what he had done with the murder weapon. The wooden stock of the spade had been discovered in undergrowth near the grave, but its metal head was still missing. Murphy admitted that he had thrown it into a nearby river. It was not an easy task to retrieve the piece of evidence, and the officers involved in the case showed great tenacity in dredging the murky waters of the river. The bloodstained head of the spade was eventually retrieved and matched to its broken handle. The implement was found to have been stolen from the shed of a farmer who sometimes employed Murphy as a casual labourer.

The trial of Stephen Murphy took place in November 1945. His guilt was undeniable, and so his defence based its arguments on the question of his mental state. Nobody could have claimed the accused man was of fully sound mind. There was a long history of serious psychological ailments in his family, and many of his close relatives had spent time in mental hospitals. From his early childhood onwards, those who came into contact with Stephen Murphy considered him eccentric, and in a previous century his neighbours might have called him 'fairy-touched' or a changeling. For most of his life, he had exhibited behavioural problems, lassitude and a general isolation from his fellow human beings. By 1945, medical science had moved on a little from 'fairy-doctoring', even in the wilds of Mayo, and these traits were recognized as the symptoms of severe mental illness. In Murphy's case, they probably indicate that he was suffering from schizophrenia, a mental illness which researchers have since discovered is unusually common in many regions of Ireland. A psychologist testifying at the trial diagnosed his disorder as dementia praecox, a term used at the time to describe a form of the disease.

Yet mental illness was not of itself considered an excuse for murder; there were other criteria to be satisfied before a guilty but insane verdict on Murphy could be justified. Ireland takes its definition of insanity as a legal defence from the same source as England, namely the M'Naghton ruling. This ruling derives from a famous murder case of the nineteenth century, when a lunatic attempted to assassinate Sir Robert Peel under the delusion there was a plot against him. In the event, he shot the wrong man, killing his target's private secretary. The most important tenet of this ruling is that a person cannot be convicted if 'by reason of insanity he did not know he was doing wrong'. Murphy's culpability was not easy to gauge, since he had made efforts to evade being caught for his crime, and seemed to be aware of its consequences. Whilst in prison on remand, he had even told a fellow prisoner that he would not be hung because the murder was unpremeditated. This fact helped convince the jury at his trial that he was legally sane. Murphy was found guilty of murder and sentenced to death.

This verdict was not entirely satisfactory, if for no other reason than the convicted man's irrational behaviour in the days after the murder. He had behaved so erratically that he could not be considered to have had any control over his actions. In a peculiar way, his perverse sexual tastes encouraged the view that he was insane. Today we understand that a significant number of human beings from all walks of life are known to sexually abuse children. Paedophilia may disgust and horrify us, but we accept as an unpleasant fact of life that there are people who indulge in such practices. But Ireland in 1945 was still an extremely puritanical country, and both the State and the Church authorities repressed the open discussion of sexual matters. Physical relations outside of marriage were frowned upon, whilst homosexuality was generally thought to be a dangerous form of mental illness. In this climate, such a rarely acknowledged perversion as paedophilia seemed to fall outside of the realms of known human behaviour. The idea that Stephen Murphy could use a child for sexual gratification, and still be sane, undermined the moral foundations that Irish society was built on.

Today it is accepted that paedophiles, such as Murphy, are fully responsible for their actions and so they should be punished like any other criminal. In Murphy's era, this conclusion had yet to be reached by Irish courts, and his conviction was quashed on appeal. At a retrial, he was found to be insane and committed to the Hospital for the Criminally Insane. It was the right verdict, although it was possibly arrived at for the wrong reason.

THE HUME STREET
ABORTIONIST

Mame Cadden has passed into Dublin folklore for her crimes, but it is probably harsh to call her a murderess. She never set out to kill her patients, although it was inevitable that her greed and recklessness in procuring miscarriages would occasionally result in their deaths. But in the Ireland of 1956, her chosen career as a backstreet abortionist made her worse than any common killer. The brash middle-aged woman with arthritic legs and a foul tongue succeeded in bringing down the wrath of an entire nation down upon her head, and found herself universally loathed.

The train of events which ended in Mame Cadden standing trial for her life began early in the morning on 18 April 1956, when a milkman found a woman's body on the pavement outside of 15 Hume Street, one of a row of Georgian houses close to St Stephen's Green, Dublin. It was immediately obvious that foul play of some sort was involved, since the body was naked from the waist down. A black overcoat had been loosely draped over it, and a woman's handbag and a parcel containing shoes were dumped on the steps of the adjacent house.

A three-foot-long mark on the dirt of the pavement nearby suggested the body had been dragged from the house next door, number 17. As the milkman looked at the body, he noticed a woman with 'fair hair raised up on her forehead, puffed' standing in the basement yard, but instead of confronting her he ran off to find a Garda. By the time he returned to the scene with a policeman, she was gone.

An autopsy showed the cause of death to be a botched abortion. The woman, identified as one Mrs Helen O'Reilly by documents in her purse, had been five months pregnant. In attempting to pump a gas or liquid into her vaginal passage, in order to cause a miscarriage, her abortionist had introduced air into her bloodstream through the placenta. This caused an embolism, which resulted in the victim's death within a few minutes. There was a strong smell of disinfectant from the womb, and the condition of her internal organs suggested somebody well experienced in these matters had performed the operation. The time of death was difficult to estimate, since the speed of the cooling of the body depended on whether she died indoors or on the street. In the first scenario, which seemed the most likely, the death of Mrs O'Reilly had occurred between 9 p.m. and midnight on the previous evening.

Police enquiries revealed that the victim, who was thirty-three years old, had only been resident in Ireland for a few weeks. Up to then, she was living with her sister in Preston, Lancashire, after separating from her husband John O'Reilly about a year previously. Although he was now living in Nigeria, John O'Reilly was familiar to the Irish police because of his activities in the Second World War, when he broadcast propaganda messages for the Nazis and was later interned after parachuting into Ireland as a German spy. Helen O'Reilly arrived in Dublin on 4 April, and then stayed around the city centre in boarding houses and with several male acquaintances. She had some money saved up, as was shown by her bank book, and appears to have supplemented this with loans from her men friends, who recalled her lively humour and sense of fun.

Mrs O'Reilly's appearance of gaiety was deceptive. She actually felt depressed and worried, as she confided to one of her boarding-house landladies. Having already given birth to six children, all of whom were at present in care or with relatives, Mrs O'Reilly was now pregnant again. It can be surmised she was in Dublin to dispose of this unwanted child, since she knew that abortions were obtainable in the city without too much difficulty. Shortly before her death Mrs O'Reilly went to her bank and withdrew a sizable sum in cash. On the night before her abortion, she moved to a boarding house in Ely Place. Her new lodgings were only forty yards from the place in Hume Street where her body was found.

The Gardai were already aware that 'illegal operations' (as abortions were euphemistically called) were available in this area. Five years previously, a young chorus girl named Edna Bird had died on Hume Street in similar circumstances to Mrs O'Reilly. It was rumoured that Miss Bird had gone home after her procured miscarriage, and later that night suddenly begun to haemorrhage. Unable to risk going to a doctor or hospital because of the danger of being arrested, the girl was returning to her abortionist for help when she collapsed and bled to death on the pavement. The chief suspect in this abortion case had escaped punishment because the Gardai could not gather enough evidence to secure a conviction.

The Gardai were convinced that the person who killed Edna Bird was also responsible for the death of Mrs O'Reilly. One of the tenants of the flats in 17 Hume Street was not only a medical practitioner of sorts, but also a qualified midwife and a convicted abortionist. Although the woman now offered a number of services, such as massages, hair treatments and enemas to her clients, her previous record made it likely she was responsible for the body left on the pavement outside of the house next door. Mary Anne 'Mame' Cadden, or Nurse Cadden as the woman living in the small upstairs flat in number 17 was usually known, was around sixty years old in 1956. Although she had lived most of her life in Ireland, her place of birth was in Pennsylvania and she could claim American citizenship. A large and fairly well-preserved woman with dyed blonde hair, she was feared by many of her acquaintances because of her fierce temper and use of strong language.

Nurse Cadden's public notoriety went back to 1939, when she was at the centre of a widely reported criminal trial. For several years, she had been running a private nursing home in the Dublin suburb of Rathmines, specializing in the care of unmarried mothers. At that time illegitimacy was such a social stigma that few women wanted to keep their babies. For a sizable fee, Cadden offered to place the unwanted infants she delivered with suitable foster couples. What her unofficial adoption agency actually did was to dump the babies out in the countryside, so they could be found by strangers and placed in State orphanages. In 1939, her distinctive two-seater sports car was recognized in Meath on one such mission, and she and a colleague were arrested for abandoning a month-old baby. The now infamous 'Nurse Cadden' was imprisoned for twelve months.

During the Emergency (as the Second World War was known in Ireland) pregnant women seeking abortions were unable to get across to England. Cadden was a member of a thriving ring of backstreet abortionists that had sprung up

in Dublin to fill the demand for illegal pregnancy termina-
tions. She had made a good living until she was convicted
in 1945 for performing an abortion on one of her clients
and sentenced to five years in gaol. After her release she
settled in Hume Street, where she offered a range of bor-
derline medical treatments. At the same time, the Gardai
were convinced that she was still carrying out her profitable
criminal activities.

The problem facing the police was not finding out who
killed Helen O'Reilly but gaining enough evidence to secure
a conviction. 'Everybody knew who did it when the body
was found' – one of the officers in the case later said – 'But it
was one thing to know it and another to prove it.' The pains-
taking methods and new techniques pioneered by the Garda
Technical Unit to link Cadden to Helen O'Reilly made the
case a classic of forensic detection. It was afterwards quoted
in the FBI manual, and used to help train investigators in
other police forces. The man who oversaw the gathering of
forensic evidence in the Cadden inquiry was Superintendent
George Lawlor, for many years the champion of scientific
detection techniques within the Gardai. In his long career, he
helped to solve dozens of Irish murders (including several
of those in this book).

The web of circumstantial evidence that enmeshed Mame
Cadden began to be spun when a policeman called at her flat
shortly after the murder. Almost the first thing he noticed
was a bucket, which emitted a strong smell of disinfectant.
When questioned by him, Cadden denied any knowledge of
Helen O'Reilly's death, and claimed she had spent most of
the previous day in bed, rising only at about 10.30 p.m. to
spend an hour with an unnamed male patient who had come
up from Kilkenny. Her neighbour, Mrs Flattery, who said

she had heard the nurse talking to two women in the afternoon, refuted this account. Later that evening, she had seen Cadden drawing water from the sink and washing clothes, whilst there had been loud noises on the landing and stairs in the early hours of the morning. Other witnesses from the house later confirmed that Cadden was up and about on the day in question, whilst a man in the house next door remembered hearing sounds on the street outside at around 5.30 a.m. – presumably the body being dragged from next door into the street.

When the Gardai returned with a warrant, Cadden was confident that she had cleaned away any incriminating evidence amd she told them, 'Search away, you will find nothing here.' In saying this, she underestimated their forensic expertise; a thorough investigation of the premises turned up a number of important clues. Detectives found two syringes, forceps (on which, it was discovered, there were traces of fresh blood), rubber sheets and two specula (surgical instruments which are used for examining women). These last items were in a hatbox, which Cadden claimed had been untouched for over a year, although there were recent hand marks on its dusty rim.

A diary with a list of Cadden's appointments intrigued George Lawlor. The clients were not named, but the entries were accompanied by short, descriptive comments that referred to each person's clothes or appearance. Amongst the numerous entries for small sums of money were two for £50 each, the type of large sum that an abortion might cost. One of these was for 17 April, the day before the discovery of Helen O'Reilly's body. It had been written in red ink, but scratched over with black until it was practically illegible. Mame Cadden, when questioned, said it read 'Blue Coat

2 p.m.' and referred to a woman to whom she had given a series of treatments for a hair condition. Lawlor was not satisfied and took the diary away for further examination.

In the hallway outside of the flat, two parallel lines in the dirt suggested that a heavy object had been dragged across the linoleum floor. A section of this was cut out for forensic examination, along with a number of hairs and fibres taken from two coconut mats in the flat. Later, a brown rabbit-skin cape and a red dressing gown belonging to Cadden were also removed to the Garda laboratory.

None of this material provided incontrovertible proof that O'Reilly had died in Cadden's flat, but it helped build up the strong case against her. A number of fibres and hairs gleaned in Nurse Cadden's house and flat were matched to those found on the dead woman's black overcoat and shoes; these included several dyed-blond hairs similar to Cadden's, and hairs from the rabbit-skin cape. Minute traces of blood, discovered on the pavement outside number 15 and on the stairs and landings of number 17, confirmed that O'Reilly's corpse was almost certainly carried from Cadden's room to the street. George Lawlor deciphered the unreadable diary entry by the use of infrared photography, believed to be the first use of a technique that is now part of standard police procedure. Beneath its overlay of dark ink it was discovered to read 'Black Coat', a clear indication that Helen O'Reilly had been Mame Cadden's patient that day. The Gardai were confident that this scientific evidence, corroborated by the testimony of her neighbours and the milkman who had found the body, would secure a conviction. They arrested the suspect.

Mame Cadden stood trial for the crime of 'murder in the course of procuring abortion' in November 1956. It may seem odd that she was accused of murder rather than manslaughter, which would appear at first sight to be the more appropriate charge. The legal reason for this stems from the Offences Against the Persons Act of 1861, which makes 'unlawfully using an instrument to procure a miscarriage' a felony. Any death caused in the course of a felony is considered murder, so that although Cadden did not intend O'Reilly's death it was legally justifiable to charge her for murder.

It should be noted that Mame Cadden was tried alone, even though she almost certainly had at least one accomplice. At her age and in her state of health, it was highly unlikely she could have dragged Helen O'Reilly down to the street by herself. Out of loyalty, or simply because she knew that naming somebody else would not lessen her own sentence, the abortionist did not implicate anybody else.

The trial was a foregone conclusion. Cadden's barrister was able to cast doubt on some of the evidence against his client by disputing the time of Helen O'Reilly's death; he also tore apart the milkman's testimony that he had seen a woman resembling his client in the basement yard of 15 Hume Street. But the prosecution's case was very strong, and the jury took less than an hour to find her guilty. The death of Helen O'Reilly had been widely reported in the newspapers, and her killer was convicted in the streets and pubs of Dublin long before she appeared in court. Cadden was so disliked that the crowd outside the courtroom clapped and cheered when the judge handed down the death penalty.

Cadden reacted angrily to her sentence. When asked why she should not receive the death penalty, she replied 'You will never do it. This is not my country . . . only for the presence of my counsel I would say something you would not like to hear.' And after the judge had put on her black cap and sentenced her to death, her response was 'Well, I am not a Catholic. Take that now!' It is to her credit that she was not afraid to defy her accusers and their moral hypocrisy. Mame Cadden has been portrayed as an amoral monster – a bad-tempered harridan who despised her unfortunate clients whilst fleecing them of their money. She was all this and more. In trying to abort Mrs O'Reilly's five-month-old foetus – an operation that would be risky even if carried out in a hospital by trained doctors – she showed that she was ruthless and unconcerned with her patient's wellbeing. Yet clients only came to backstreet abortionists like her because they had no alternative. Unmarried mothers were ostracized, forced to give up their children, and even locked away in religious institutions to be 'reformed'. The Dubliners who so rejoiced at Cadden's fall contributed to her crimes, by their complicity in Irish society's tyrannical treatment of single women who became pregnant.

There was little likelihood that Mame Cadden's death penalty would be carried out, since no woman had been hanged in Ireland since 1925. In due course, she was re-prieved and sentenced to life imprisonment. Towards the end of 1958, Cadden developed psychological problems and was transferred to the Hospital for the Criminally Insane at Dundrum, County Dublin, where her health declined rapidly. She died in April 1959, almost exactly three years after the fatal abortion of Helen O'Reilly.

'THE FIELD' MURDER

A crime must be very serious to draw the wrath of the Catholic hierarchy upon itself, especially in the Ireland of forty years ago, where the Church still had a tremendous hold over the people. Yet, in March 1960, the Bishop of Tralee, Dr Moynihan, imposed severe spiritual penalties following an unsolved murder in his diocese. 'Over a year ago there was the murder of Maurice Moore of Reamore, a God-fearing harmless man,' he said. 'On his way home from the house of a neighbour he was foully done to death . . . nobody suspects that the murderer of Maurice Moore came from miles away . . . the murderer is a native of that district somewhere . . . Now if it is not too late I make this public appeal to any people who can throw any light on the murder of Maurice Moore to tell what they know to the civic guards.'

The murder of Moss Moore remains unsolved in police files, despite the widely held belief that his neighbour, Dan Foley, killed him. Why nobody was ever convicted for the murder is a more controversial question than the identity of the killer, since everybody in the region knew who had committed it, and why. The failure to apprehend Dan Foley made for an unsatisfactory conclusion to one of the strangest of Irish murder stories. How could a minor quarrel over land between two law-abiding neighbours culminate with the brutal murder of one good man by another?

Reamore, the mountainous district on whose slopes these events took place, lies a few miles north of Tralee, County

Kerry. It is poor farm country, and in the 1950s was inhabited by a community of hill farmers, who eked a living out of their smallholdings of a few dozen acres each. Anybody who has ever lived amidst such folk will tell you that they are 'a law unto themselves' – independent, proud and self-sufficient. Although neighbourliness is amongst their strongest qualities, when neighbours fall out their feuds can last for generations. Fifty years ago, Reamore – the name means 'the Big Rough' or 'Wasteland' – was still an isolated and backward area by normal standards. Television had not yet arrived in Ireland, farmers brought their milk to the local creamery on horse-drawn carts, and life still moved to the slow traditional rhythms of the countryside.

Moss Moore, a bachelor farmer, was a typical smallholder of that era. He was forty-six years old at the time of his death, and owned twenty-five acres of land (about half of which was bog) on the side of the mountain. He lived in a simple two-room stone cottage on his farm, and grew a few vegetables and potatoes in a plot nearby. The remainder of his property, excluding the rough lands, was given over to pasture and supported four cows, two pigs and a horse to draw the owner's cart. Moore also had a cat, a greyhound and a black-and-white collie named Smallie. He was almost inseparable from his two dogs, and had to lock them in his cottage when he went out at night, to stop them following him. On a material level, it was a poor existence for any man, but Moss Moore seems to have been quite contented with his lifestyle. A quick-tongued and gregarious character, he was a popular member of his little community, and regularly attended the card-games and church functions that were the main social entertainment in the neighbourhood.

Dan Foley, Moss's nearest neighbor, lived with his wife

and her invalid brother about forty yards further up the hillside. Their house lay on the other side of a stream that rushed down from the mountain in a six-foot deep ravine, and formed the boundary between the two farms. A powerfully built and somewhat silent man in his early sixties, he had been deeply involved in the Independence Movement against the British. He was respected and even feared by his neighbours in Reamore, who knew he had a ferocious temper and could be a dangerous man to cross. But despite this reputation, he enjoyed good relations with the whippet-like Moore, at least until the summer of 1958, and would often help the smaller man out with some of the heavier physical jobs on his farm, such as cutting turf for burning from their adjacent patches of bog. The bachelor responded by carrying out the small errands and favours that are expected between neighbours in the Irish countryside.

The dispute that caused the escalating feud between the two farmers, and finally led to their homicidal confrontation on the rain-swept hillside, began with a row over a fence. Dan Foley's small herd of cattle was in the habit of wandering off his pastures into the dangerous bogs that hemmed in the property of the two farmers. He feared that his animals might be injured and decided to run a fence along the edge of his land to keep them in. The older man, after discussing his problem with Moss Moore, placed the barrier on a hard ridge of land that rose slightly above the marshy fields. He considered this to be the natural boundary between his land and his neighbours.

Moss Moore was furious when he saw the fence, which he claimed had been built several yards inside his property. In his estimation, Foley had encroached upon almost an acre of his small farm, as well as cutting off his access to his turf-cutting in the bog. Moore demanded that the fence be removed at once, failing which he would take legal action.

Any other words that may have passed between the two erstwhile friends have not been recorded, but Moore had a cutting tongue on occasion. His sarcastic comments must have enraged his neighbour, since afterwards the two men stopped talking altogether, and would not acknowledge each other when they met on the road or in the village. Their bitter quarrel was common knowledge in Reamore, and the parish priest and their many mutual friends tried to bring them together to sort out the problem. Neither would be reconciled to the other, or agree to make any concession over the position of the disputed fence. By the autumn of 1958, Dan Foley and Moss Moore had become sworn enemies over the festering disagreement, and were taking legal action against each other. A date to hear the case was set for December in the district court in Tralee. Foley, whose legal position was weaker than Moore's, was heard to say, 'Only one of us will be going down to hear it.'

Around this time, Moore began to tell his friends that he suspected Foley planned to attack him, and was stalking him when he came home at night. He showed them a stout walking stick he was carrying to beat off the stronger man if necessary. Foley had warned his neighbour to stay off his land, causing Moore a major problem since the path to his cottage followed the ravine up Foley's side of the river. Ten days before his death, the worried bachelor farmer contacted Detective Kavanagh at the Tralee Garda Station, who was friendly with both him and Dan Foley. He told the policeman he was in danger, and begged him to come to Reamore and warn his neighbour off. Kavanagh felt it would be unethical to intervene in what had become a civil matter, and placated the little farmer with vague promises.

On the night of Thursday 6 November 1958, Moss Moore went to the weekly card game at Miss Julie Collin's house. At the end of the evening, he left with an acquaintance named Paul Reidy, who walked him along the road to the narrow track leading up the ravine to the cottage. Moore said goodbye to his friend and walked off into the darkness; he was wearing a tweed overcoat and carried a stick in one hand and a bicycle lamp in the other. He was never seen alive again, except by the man who murdered him. Two days later, his friends became worried about his failure to turn up at the creamery. Paul Reidy and some other neighbours walked up to the cottage to make sure the farmer had not been taken ill. They found the front door locked, and Moore's two dogs running free in the yard. When they looked at the latch more carefully they saw it was hanging loose. Some unknown hand had torn it off, afterwards roughly reattaching the lock onto the door. Reidy entered the cottage and discovered it to be empty; there was nothing to suggest that Moore had returned there after the card game.

The police in Tralee were notified and immediately began a search of the area around Moore's farm. News spread about the hunt for the missing man, and curious onlookers began turning up from all over Kerry and the adjoining counties. There were so many people trampling around Moss Moore's property that they destroyed any hope of finding forensic evidence in his yard or cottage. The Gardai arranged for a missing persons appeal to be broadcast on the radio and also published by the national newspapers, but there was no response. The search of the hillside, hampered by heavy rain, went on for days without success.

It was decided to involve the Garda Technical Unit, popularly known as the 'murder squad', and Superintendent George Lawlor was dispatched to the scene. At his suggestion, the local Gardai undertook a further search of the ravine, which divided Moore's farm from Foley's. On 15 November, nine days after Moss Moore's disappearance, Sergeant Michael Costelloe found a cap while probing along the overgrown bank of the river. A few yards further along, he made a gruesome discovery; sticking out of the stream, where it had been hidden by the water gushing down the mountainside after the heavy rain, was the top of a booted leg.

The crouched body of Moss Moore, with its hands still up and fists clenched to fight off an attacker, had been hidden in a small cave in the riverbank. Someone who had an intimate knowledge of the area must have placed it there. Moss Moore's corpse was so tightly wedged into the narrow aperture that the Gardai had to dig it out. Moore's face had been severely battered, and detectives later surmised that he had been throttled with his own walking stick. The broken pieces of the weapon were found nearby. His bicycle lamp was not at the scene, but was later discovered buried in the cabbage patch beside the cottage. The murderer, who had gone to Moore's cottage after killing his victim, had presumably concealed it there.

The Gardai believed that he had released the dogs after breaking down the front door. It was recalled afterwards by local people involved in the search, that these faithful animals had lingered for days on the ravine above the cave where Moore's body was hidden. Three weeks later, the collie, Smallie, briefly achieved national fame when he escaped from his new owners, and walked eight miles to return to his dead master's cottage.

Moss Moore's funeral was the largest in the history of the district. His hearse was followed to the local graveyard at Reamore Cross by a funeral cortege over one and a half miles long. The mourners included Foley, who was the only suspect in the case. The Gardai had closely questioned the farmer, but his wife said he had not left their house on the evening of the murder. Regrettably there was no forensic evidence to disprove this alibi, and link him directly to the attack on Moore. Even so, the known enmity between the men should have been enough to form the basis of a strong circumstantial case against Dan Foley.

What happened (or rather didn't happen) next remains a matter of some controversy. Although a file was sent to the Director of Public Prosecutions, no charges were laid against the suspect. Foley, it was whispered in Reamore, had powerful friends in the ruling Fianna Fáil Party – old comrades, who had served with him in the Independence War, and now held high political positions, were now shielding him from prosecution. Other rumours claimed that certain people in the district were withholding important information, despite repeated requests by their priests for them to contact the police. There was probably some degree of truth in both allegations. On the other hand, the case against Dan Foley was not strong in many respects. The police lacked the one vital witness, or piece of evidence, that might turn their suspicions of his guilt into a successful prosecution. Foley was never charged in connection with the death of Moss Moore, who officially remains the victim of an unsolved murder.

Nevertheless, the farmer served a sentence of sorts for his crime. He became an isolated outcast in Reamore, and was shunned by many of his neighbours. Shots were fired into his house, and a bomb exploded beside his gable wall. Dan Foley died from natural causes in 1963, only a few years after the murder of his enemy. Normally he would have been buried in the family plot at Reamore Cross, in the same graveyard as Moss Moore. Instead, his family interred his body five miles away in Tralee. His house was abandoned after the deaths of his wife and her brother some years later, and has since been demolished. Moss Moore's cottage had already been knocked down. Nothing now remains of the farms but the memory of two ordinary Irish countrymen, both of whose lives were destroyed in a squabble over a few square yards of marshy field.

The suspected murder of Moss Moore by Dan Foley strongly impressed itself on an aspiring young playwright named John B. Keane. The story inspired the Listowel publican, who was acquainted with both men, to write 'The Field', one of the finest Irish plays of the twentieth century. Its protagonist, Bull McCabe, is a farmer who commits murder to acquire a piece of land that he believes should be his by right.

A DEATH IN MURDERING HOLLOW

It sometimes happens that a murderer escapes punishment even though the police are sure of his guilt. Perhaps he flees before his arrest, or is convicted and then released on a technicality. The circumstances surrounding the unsolved murder of Celia McEvoy were different. The Gardai came within a hairsbreadth of making an arrest, and then lost their suspect in the most distressing circumstances.

The case began on the morning of 6 November 1962, when the body of a young woman was found on the out-skirts of the town of Port Laoise. The victim was identified as Cecilia McEvoy, a twenty-two-year-old hotel worker who was home from Dublin on a short holiday. She lay half-concealed in the undergrowth of an area of rough land known locally as 'Murdering Hollow'. Miss McEvoy, whose family lived not far away in the Stradbally area, had been strangled. There was no sign of rape, and she was fully dressed. Robbery could also be discounted as a motive, although the murderer had taken the woman's shoes and handbag.

Cecilia McEvoy had last been seen alive on the previ-ous evening about 6 p.m., when she left her family home in Stradbally. She was planning to hitch a lift into Port Laoise, and then go to the cinema. There was no evidence that she reached the town, and the Gardai were fairly sure her killer had picked her up on the road in from Stradbally.

This was confirmed when her autopsy placed the time of death at around 10 p.m. Fortunately the Stradbally–Port Laoise road had been fairly busy that night. Several car drivers and pedestrians, who knew the victim, contacted the Gardai to inform them they had seen her with a man in a small car. The police were less lucky in tracing the occupants of four vehicles that were parked in the vicinity of Murdering Hollow around the hour of the murder. Not one of them came forward, despite repeated appeals. The spot was a popular meeting place for clandestine lovers, and it may be assumed that the four drivers and their passengers had reasons of their own for keeping their identities a secret.

The Gardai, despite this minor setback, were making good progress in solving the murder. They were interested in one particular suspect, and were urgently seeking the car in which the victim had been a passenger. From this vehicle, if it could be traced, they hoped to obtain evidence that would place its driver on the murder scene. A set of tyre tracks, with a distinctive tread, had been found beside the clump of undergrowth; if detectives could match these to the suspect's car, they had their man. However, the murderer was alerted to the existence of this most telling piece of evidence against him through the activities of a press photographer on the day after the murder. Because the photographer had been some distance away and was using a telephoto lens, the police at the murder scene did not notice him taking pictures of their forensic experts at work. One of these pictures, showing the forensic detectives making a plaster cast of the tyre tracks, was published in the next edition of the local newspaper. It emerged afterwards that the major suspect in the case bought new tyres for his car shortly afterwards, and burnt the old set.

Witnesses had identified this man as the car driver with whom they had seen Miss McEvoy on the evening of her murder. The Gardai, after interviewing the suspect at home, brought him into Port Laoise for a more thorough interrogation. Superintendent Murphy, the officer in charge of the case, confronted the suspect with the various pieces of evidence against him. Following long hours of sustained questioning, his alibi was in ribbons and by midnight he appeared to be on the on the verge of admitting his guilt. However he was exhausted, having been in custody for nearly twelve hours. There was a possibility that he might withdraw his confession later, on the grounds that it had been illegally obtained under duress. Superintendent Murphy told him to go home and have a good night's sleep before continuing the interview the following morning.

The Gardai were confident that the suspect would sign a confession when he returned. But they had not reckoned on the suspect's fear of being publicly revealed as the murderer of Cecilia McEvoy. When the man left the Garda station, he ignored the road that led to his house. Instead, he drove off to a nearby bog and drowned himself in a pool of water.

'A WOMAN TAINTED'

Comparatively few Irish murders can be attributed to sexual jealousy – indeed it is a much less common motive for taking a human life than might be expected. Some observers attribute this fact to Ireland's cold and damp weather, which they say leaves its people less hot-blooded than the peoples of warmer climates. This idea is nonsensical no doubt, but it must be said that what the French call the 'crime of passion' is a rare occurrence on Irish shores. There was, nevertheless, a tragic example of this kind of crime in Dublin in 1964. It involved two young people from diverse cultural backgrounds, whose romance ended in disaster because of the different attitudes held by their respective cultures towards the relationship between the sexes. The murder of Hazel Mullen by Indian student, Shan Mohangi, was fuelled by rage at what he considered to be an unforgivable sexual betrayal on her part. Yet it can be argued that his jealousy sprang partly from the failure of his future wife to meet the strict standards expected of women in his own society. Mohangi's misplaced idealization of marriage cost a vibrant young Irish woman her life.

His victim, Hazel Mullen, was the fourth child in a family of eight. She was only fourteen years old in August 1962, when she first met Shan Mohangi in a chemist's shop where she was working. The handsome twenty-two-year-old medical student was her first boyfriend, and within days the young couple were deeply in love. Mohangi became a regular visitor at Hazel's home in Shankill, County Dublin, where her mother, a widow whose husband had died the previous year, was won over by his charm and good manners. It should be stated that Mohangi's intentions towards the lovely young Dubliner were totally honourable – from the beginning of their involvement he wished to make her his bride. Mrs Mullen, a sensible woman, felt that her daughter was too young for such a long-term relationship. She thought that Hazel should enjoy herself, and meet other young men before settling down to the duties of wedded life. This clashed with the desires of Mohangi, in whose Indian culture marriage at an early age is quite normal.

The most unpleasant side of Mohangi's character was his possessiveness. As Hazel Mullen soon discovered, it could occasionally flare into spontaneous outbursts of violence. The medical student did not tell his new girlfriend that he had previously been engaged to a nurse. Mohangi met this young woman in 1961, shortly after he arrived from South Africa to study medicine at the College of Surgeons in Dublin. The turbulent relationship between the son of a wealthy Indian family and his first fiancée was marred by his fits of jealousy. The woman broke off the affair in July 1962 and left Dublin.

Mohangi's tendency to lose control emotionally was soon manifested during his new relationship with Hazel Mullen, although he was not usually aggressive towards her. On the first occasion, the student slapped his girlfriend's face, after she told him he was not the first man to kiss her. In a second, more serious, tantrum he threw a pot of boiling rice across the kitchen. It struck Hazel on the back and burnt her so badly that she was in hospital for three weeks. Early in 1964, Hazel informed her boyfriend that she did not want to go out with him anymore. This was a hard blow for the student, who was going through a rough patch in his life. His studies were going badly, and he was finding it impossible to survive on the meagre allowance he received from his father. His financial situation, at least, was alleviated when he was offered a job in the Green Tureen, a restaurant in the same building in Harcourt Street as his one-room apartment. His landlord, Cecil Frew, who had become something of a surrogate parent to the personable young Indian, obtained this position for him.

Hazel Mullen, meanwhile, was blossoming into womanhood. After a few months' separation, she began going out with Mohangi again, and on the surface their romance seemed stronger than ever. Yet all was not well between the couple. On her sixteenth birthday, she had taken up a new job in a bank, which enhanced her growing independence and sense of self-esteem. Her likeable personality and exceptional good looks, moreover, were attracting the interest of other men. Mohangi had renewed his liaison with his former fiancée during their separation, and continued secretly dating her even after he was reunited with Hazel (although in his eyes it was Hazel's duty as his future bride to be chaste and devoted to him at all times). Hazel's natural wish to spread her wings a little offended Mohangi's puritanical attitude towards her, and drove him to distraction. Given his volatile temperament, it placed the young woman in grave personal danger.

On Saturday 17 August, Hazel Mullen left work at lunchtime, and then disappeared. When she did not come home for dinner that evening, the Mullen family became concerned, and her brother went to see Shan Mohangi, who was working in the Green Tureen that night. The medical student said he had not seen Hazel, although they had spoken on the phone during the day. She had mentioned, the Indian said, that she intended going shopping during the afternoon. The two men went back to Shankill and informed the local Garda station that she was missing. Afterwards, Mohangi went to Hazel's home, where he stayed overnight in her bedroom. Next day, the Gardai began investigating Hazel's disappearance. In the course of their inquiries, two officers called at the Green Tureen and checked the basement; it was strewn with rubbish but otherwise appeared empty.

A strange incident had taken place in Harcourt Street on the afternoon of the previous day. A couple walking by the Green Tureen noticed smoke pouring out of a grate outside the closed restaurant. They knocked on the door to warn the occupants of the building, and a 'coloured' man answered it. Although he told them everything was all right, his demeanour raised the couple's suspicions, and they called the fire brigade. Three fire engines were dispatched to the Green Tureen, where firemen found Mohangi, naked to the waist and sweating profusely. The student explained there had been a minor fire, and showed them some smouldering rags in the basement. The firemen looked around to satisfy themselves that the blaze was extinguished, and then left.

On Sunday, Cecil Frew noticed a bad odour was permeating the restaurant, and cleared out the drains. His efforts failed to get rid of the sickly stench. The landlord was also worried about the mental health of his young Indian friend, who was obviously under great strain. Some of Mohangi's comments led Frew to suspect that his tenant was not admitting all that he knew about Hazel's disappearance. He sat down with the young man, who was very distressed, and persuaded him to contact the police and confess to murdering Hazel. Mohangi promised to wait in his apartment, and Frew went off to speak with detectives in the Harcourt Street Garda Station. When he returned with the officers, they found the medical student's door was locked. Mohangi had attempted to gas himself and was unconscious. He was rushed to the nearest hospital, where he recovered after a few days.

The dismembered remains of Hazel Mullen were hidden in the rubbish in the Green Tureen's basement, and behind a cupboard in the medical student's room. The inner organs had disappeared, and Mohangi had attempted to incinerate the victim's head so she could not be identified. The body had been dissected with a knife and cleaver. The large splashes of blood and traces of human remains found on the premises indicated the operation had been performed in an almost manic rush. There was no evidence to determine the cause of death, although it was significant that Mohangi had cut out and burnt the voice box.

In Mohangi's confession, he told of the events that led up to the death of his girlfriend. After Hazel arrived at the Green Tureen to meet him for lunch on Saturday afternoon, he asked her whether she was going out with another man. A more experienced woman would probably have deflected the question or simply lied, but the young girl was honest. She admitted – in Mohangi's own words – to having had 'something to do with somebody else'. Consumed with jealousy, he put his hands round her throat and squeezed it. When he recovered his senses, he was horrified to find that she was dead. He went to his room to try and gather his nerves. All that came to his mind was to dispose of her body, which he proceeded to cut up in a blind panic.

The young Indian's state of mind when he attacked Hazel Mullen was a vital issue in deciding whether he was guilty of murder or manslaughter. In a suicide note to his ex-fiancée he wrote 'I did not intend killing Hazel. The moment I learnt she was unfaithful to me, I lost my head and did something rash which I am regretting now.' Perhaps this was so, but as the judge pointed out at his trial in February 1964, the term 'malice aforethought' does not imply advance planning of a crime. If Mohangi wanted to kill his girlfriend for even a moment when he placed his hands around her neck, then he had murdered her. The jury decided there had been this intention, and found the student guilty of murder. He was sentenced to life imprisonment.

When the sentence came to be appealed, however, another legal point was raised. During his original trial his ex- girlfriend had testified to Mohangi's jealousy and fits of rage. She stated that he had once caught her around the throat and threatened to strangle her. The nurse further damaged Mohangi's case when she revealed Mohangi had spent the night before the murder with her. The judge's failure to direct the jury to ignore these statements, since they were irrelevant to Mohangi's guilt or innocence, was deemed prejudicial to his defence. At his second trial in July 1965, he was given the benefit of the doubt, and found guilty on the lesser charge of manslaughter. He served four years of his seven-year sentence before being released from prison, and returning to his family in South Africa.

It is questionable whether the verdict of manslaughter was correct in this case. Many men have been imprisoned or hanged for killings every bit as impulsive as the one that took the life of Hazel Mullen. On the other hand, Shan Mohangi was only a young man, and had fallen foul of the law in a strange country. This brought him some sympathy. His crime was the result of his obsessive love for his girlfriend, and if the medical student's rage was deplorable, it was not altogether within his control. Within his own self-centred emotional world, based on Indian attitudes towards women and their role, he felt he had been utterly betrayed. 'I had been prepared to give up everything at home and yet she had let me down,' he explained to the Gardai, as if it excused his anger. Perhaps the prosecution barrister best summed up the seeds of disaster that were always present in Shan Mohangi's passion for his beautiful Irish fiancée: 'From the moment the accused man formed the intention of marrying her,' he said at the first trial 'this girl was doomed either to death or serious injury. In his eyes, a woman kissed is a woman tainted.'

A FALSE CONFESSION?

When anybody begins a sentence by saying 'On mature reflection . . . ' you can be sure they are about to change a statement they made earlier. It is an expression that could be used in court at times, when men in the dock retract confessions they have already signed. The commonest grounds for such a withdrawal are that the statement was made under duress of one sort or another. Modern police forces have learnt from past mistakes to respect the legal rights of suspects, and are careful to follow the guidelines laid down for questioning them. Yet police intimidation is not the only reason given by men on trial for denying their sworn statements. The suspect in the Peggy Flynn case voluntarily admitted to murdering her, then later claimed that he only confessed because he was suffering from a psychological disorder at the time.

The body of Peggy Flynn was found on the beach at Sandymount Point, about six miles south of Dublin, on the morning of 6 February 1966. The dead woman, a thirty-nine-year-old prostitute, had been strangled with one of her stockings and a scarf. Apart from this she was fully dressed, although her handbag and shoes were missing. The Gardai soon discovered that she had last been seen on the previous evening, touting for clients on St Stephen's Green. They broadcast an appeal for any witnesses who had seen her during the evening, and discovered she had been a passenger in a white Triumph Herald car with a distinctive black trim. The detectives working the case began to trace and interview the drivers of any cars that answered this description.

One of these vehicles was owned by a young man who had since enlisted in the British Army, and was serving in the Parachute Regiment. In September 1966, whilst talking to his girlfriend, he suddenly broke down and confessed he had killed 'a bloody old woman'. He then told his story to the doctors in a British military hospital, and was placed in a psychiatric unit. The Gardai were informed of his statements, and in October the detectives investigating the murder of Peggy Flynn interviewed him in England. The suspect was eager to talk about the murder. He stated that on the night in question he had picked up Peggy Flynn in the city centre, shortly after leaving a party. They began arguing over how much he should pay her, and he lost his temper when she asked for a larger sum than he had agreed to pay. He tried to throttle the woman with his bare hands, but found he lacked the strength to kill her. The young man removed one of her stockings and her scarf, and used these as ligatures to finish her off. When she was dead, he drove out to Sandycove and left the corpse on the seashore, hoping it would be washed away by the tide.

This confession, on the face of it, seemed to wrap the case up neatly. The suspect's statement was corroborated by the theories of the Gardai, and Peggy Flynn's injuries were consistent with the young soldier's description of his assault on her. There were, nonetheless, some worrying discrepancies in the suspect's account. He said that Peggy Flynn was sober, although she had consumed large quantities of alcohol in the hours before her death. The detectives did not know what to make of his suggestion that the prostitute must have held her liquor well, since he did not notice she was drunk.

According to her friends, Peggy Flynn had been drinking heavily in a pub for hours before going to St Stephen's Green. The suspect also seemed unaware that the victim's bag and her shoes were missing, which was puzzling if he had really killed her. The detectives also took note of the suspect's mental state, and decided to confront him with these inconsistencies before finishing the interview. They pointed out he could easily have concocted his story from articles he had read in the Irish newspapers. The suspect continued to insist he had murdered Peggy Flynn.

The earlier statements he had made to British Army personnel corroborated his confession, indicating the young soldier was probably telling the truth. He was extradited back to Ireland and charged with the murder of Peggy Flynn. But once he got home, the suspect changed his mind, and said he had fabricated the whole story. Apart from the confession, there was very little evidence to implicate him, and his trial in March 1968 was dominated by the question of its veracity. Mr Martin, the defence barrister, pointed out that it was not uncommon for psychiatric patients to falsely confess to crimes they did not commit. After deliberating for four hours, the jury in the case decided the young soldier's earlier statements that he killed Peggy Flynn were unreliable. He was declared not guilty and released from custody.

AN ABDUCTION IN SLIGO

Many policemen say that child murders are the worst cases of all to investigate. When a child is slain, the reverberations stretch out like the ripples of a wave, carrying fear and anguish far beyond the victim's immediate friends and family. The crimes are often accompanied by sordid or pathetic details that prey on the mind, while media pressure for a quick arrest adds to the pressure on the detectives assigned to the inquiry.

In Ireland, as in every country in the world, there are various types of child murder, with a wide spectrum of motives. The most difficult to solve are those where a stranger abducts and sexually abuses his victim. Child sex-killers are notoriously difficult to track down (although over the last decade DNA testing has helped make the task a little easier), and the investigation into the murder of ten-year-old Bernadette Connolly in 1970 was particularly frustrating for the Gardai. The detectives involved in the case worked themselves into the ground, but from beginning to end they were plagued with bad luck. There were other factors that hampered the police from following one potentially significant lead, and the lack of cooperation they received from certain quarters still leaves a bad taste in the mouth.

Bernadette Connolly disappeared late in the afternoon of Friday 17 April 1970, while cycling between her home at Collooney, County Sligo, and a friend's house a few miles away. Later that evening, the splashdown of the Apollo

Moon Mission was broadcast on television, providing an easy point of reference for witnesses trying to remember the day. Her abandoned bicycle was discovered about a mile away from her destination, triggering off a massive search that encompassed a large area of northwestern Ireland. Initially the Gardai concentrated on interviewing potential witnesses, and tried to match a single adult fingerprint left on the crossbar of the missing child's bicycle. During the first weeks of the investigation, over five hundred local people and known sex offenders were fingerprinted without success. Three men had been working in their fields near to the site of the abduction, but none of them remembered seeing the missing girl. A public appeal for help prompted a number of people who had been driving on the road to contact the police. The Gardai, after comparing their statements, became interested in two vehicles whose drivers had yet to come forward – a green van and a large dark car.

The Gardai were unable to trace the car, but found that St Joseph's Retreat, a Passionist Monastery in Clonmahon, County Sligo, possessed a van similar to the one they were seeking. They visited the monastery and found out that its whereabouts could not be accounted for between 4.30 p.m. and 7.30 p.m. on the day that Bernadette Connolly went missing. There were twenty-two priests and three farm workers resident at the time, any one of whom might have taken the vehicle.

After further inquiries, the police talked to an attendant at a nearby petrol station. He named a priest at the monastery, and stated he had bought petrol for the green van between 7 p.m. and 8 p.m. on 17 April. The priest in question denied this, and said that he had last purchased petrol there on the morning of 16 April. The two men were brought together, but, since neither would change their story, the Gardai had to let the matter go.

Several months went by, and as other serious crimes took up their attention the Gardai wound down the inquiry. Then, out of the blue, the partially clothed corpse of the abducted child was accidentally discovered in early August. The murderer had buried his victim in a bog at Limnagh, County Roscommon, about fifteen miles away from Collooney. The body was badly decomposed, and it was impossible to determine a cause of death. Any other forensic evidence or clues that the grave might provide had rotted away in the damp soil. Luck had again been with the killer. The Gardai were told about the newly dug patch of earth a few days after the disappearance. They had sent an officer out to search the bog, but he could not find it.

The Gardai, even though the trail was cold, renewed their efforts. They fingerprinted 2,500 potential suspects in the Roscommon–Sligo region, but once again their hard work failed to turn up a match to the fingerprint on the bicycle. Then, towards the end of August, the local Garda in Collooney was chatting to one of the Connolly family's neighbours. The man – who had a cast iron alibi for the kidnapping – casually mentioned he had lifted Bernadette's bike into the boot of his car shortly before she was abducted. The print on the crossbar was found to be his, negating the months of work spent in eliminating suspects through their fingerprints. After this setback, it is hardly surprising that the Gardai never solved the case, though it was certainly not for want of trying.

The questions concerning the possible involvement of the van from St Joseph's Retreat were never properly resolved, and the priests and staff at the monastery could not be eliminated from the inquiry. It sometimes appeared that whenever the officers raised questions about this vehicle, they confronted a wall of dissimulation. On the Gardai's initial visit to the monastery, for example, nobody could give an alibi to the priest mentioned by the garage attendant but a fortnight later two witness stated he was watching the return of the moon-landing during the relevant hours. In the months after the murder, the Gardai were told that two men in the vicinity of the abduction had spoken of seeing the green van at the abduction site, although both had concealed this fact during their interviews. They were questioned again, but denied ever having made the comments. None of the above proves anything. The human memory is imperfect and witnesses are sometimes mistaken. Now and then they even lie, or make up stories for malicious reasons of their own. Nevertheless one cannot help feeling that a cocoon of silence was woven around the activities of the monastery's green van on that day. If local people were reluctant to implicate a Catholic priest, it is hardly surprising. In 1970, the authority of the Church was much stronger than today, and it was not acceptable to accuse a clergyman of the rape and murder of a child.

One further point suggests that the killer of Bernadette Connolly came from the general locality of Sligo. Seven years later, a second child went missing in circumstances that closely resembled the Collooney abduction. On 18 March 1977, a Bank Holiday weekend, seven-year-old Mary Doyle disappeared while visiting her grandparents near Ballyshannon in County Donegal. The child was never found, despite a search every bit as extensive as that for Bernadette Connolly. Mary Doyle's mother believed that her daughter was taken into a mysterious car that she saw near the grandparents' farmhouse that day. The police were unable to trace it. Ballyshannon is only about forty miles north of Collooney. If the two incidents were connected, there can be little doubt that a dangerous child-killer was at large in the northwest of Ireland during those years – a killer who has never been caught.

THE MURDERING WOMEN

It is often supposed that the many acts of violence committed in Northern Ireland during the Troubles were the actions of men and youths. Although the great majority indeed were, there were also a number of horrific acts committed by women against other women, usually members of their own community. The death in July 1974 of Ann Ogilby, a Protestant woman from the Sandy Row district of central Belfast, was one chilling example.

Grass cutters found her body at 9 a.m. on 29 July in a ditch by the verge of the M1 motorway, about half a mile from its end and where it enters Belfast. The body was lying partly in the water of the ditch, but it was clear from its state and from the grass underneath, that it had lain there unnoticed for several days. A shoe, missing from the body, and a large sack, were found close by. At that time, the police had had no notification of any missing person and the body could not be identified. Post-mortem examination showed that the woman, in her late twenties, had received massive and deep head injuries. In addition, there was evidence of severe bruising to her arms and legs. It was clear that she had been the victim of a sustained and brutal assault.

Following the circulation of a description of the murdered woman, carried on radio and TV news bulletins, the Royal Ulster Constabulary (RUC) were contacted by a Belfast social worker. One of the social worker's 'clients' was an unmarried mother named Ann Ogilby. She had been missing since 24 July, when she had arrived late for an appointment at the Social Services centre in Lower Crescent. She then left again before the social worker had seen her. One of her children, six-year-old Sharlene, was with her (her other three children, all younger, were in council care). Later the same day, Sharlene was left at the YWCA Hostel on the city's Malone Road, where she and her mother were staying. No one had seen her mother since that day, and Sharlene was now being cared for in a children's home.

Soon the police were able to piece together the bleak story of Ann Ogilby's life. She had been living in Belfast for about six years, coming originally from a small County Tyrone village, and had drifted from address to address, her successive pregnancies due to casual sexual relationships. She was well known to the Social Services staff, who had arranged for her to be accommodated at the YWCA. The reason for her murder was still a mystery.

At this point, there was an astonishing discovery. A police sergeant from the Queen Street Police Station, who had been on duty in the city centre on Wednesday 23 July, had actually seen and spoken to Ann Ogilby on that day and on the following day. It had been he who brought her to the Social Services centre, for the appointment she ultimately failed to keep.

The sergeant had been called to the bus station in Glengall Street, where staff told him they had witnessed a young woman being dragged out of a bus by a group of women, and driven away in a car. The sergeant put a description of the car out over his radio, and it was duly intercepted by a police vehicle on its way out of the city, on the Upper Malone Road. The police were surprised to find ten women squeezed into the one car. Some of the passengers claimed they were on their way to a party. When asked who was the one who had been taken off the bus, Ann Ogilby identified herself and all ten were taken back to Queen Street. Although the RUC sergeant found Ann Ogilby to be in a somewhat distressed condition, she refused to make any complaint, and no charges (with the possible exception of dangerous driving) could be brought. But all the women's names and addresses – the majority from the Sandy Row area – had been noted and checked. The sergeant arranged for Ann Ogilby to return to the station next day when she again refused to make any charge against the other women. It was then that the sergeant drove her to the Social Services centre in Lower Crescent.

Meanwhile, the CID officers assigned to the case had had the difficult task of interviewing the victim's six-year-old daughter. Fortunately, Sharlene was a composed and intelligent little girl who was able not only to describe the visit to the Social Services centre, but also to direct the police to the place where she and her mother had been taken. A man driving a blue van had come for them, and driven them to a building in Hunter Street, just by Sandy Row. The man had unlocked the door to the building and they had gone in, followed by a group of women wearing face masks. He had then given Sharlene ten pence to go to the corner shop and buy sweets. When the child came back with her sweets, the man put her back into the van, drove her to the YWCA hostel, rang the bell, and left her on the doorstep.

The building was a former bakery, now a clubhouse for the UDA (Ulster Defence Association). Events continued to happen at a rapid pace. The day after the building was identified, the RUC arrested the nine women who had been identified after the bus station incident. They raided the club building and found, in a dismal and decrepit upstairs room, essential items of evidence. Beside an old wooden bench were a matchbox, some pieces of wood, and a sack, all stained with blood. Beneath the sack were a number of blood-stained documents including Ann Ogilby's National Insurance card and an envelope bearing the address 'W. J. Young, No 40, Maze Prison, Lisburn'. With it was a slip of paper on which had been written: 'Change pass from Monday to Tuesday, Compound 9, W. J. Young, 182784.'

Armed with these items, it was easy for the investigators to commence a productive line of questioning. The forensic science lab confirmed that the bloodstains in the upper room matched Ann Ogilby's blood group. Young was a Loyalist prisoner held in the Maze. Although he was married, he had been living with Ann Ogilby for several months before his arrest, and she had continued to visit him in prison. There had been friction between her and his wife. Mrs Young, the prisoner's wife, had been receiving UDA money to send food parcels to her husband, and Ann Ogilby had complained that Mrs Young had been misusing these funds. The resultant row had led to Ann Ogilby being questioned by the Sandy Row women's section of the UDA, under its head, Elizabeth Douglas. This had happened on the evening of 23 July, and it was a sarcastic comment made by Ann Ogilby as they dropped her afterwards at the Glengall Street bus station that had led to their pulling her out of the bus. The timely action of the police had fortuitously saved her that evening. However, Elizabeth Douglas and her group decided that she should receive a punishment beating. Knowing of her appointment at the Social Services centre in Lower Crescent, they sent one Albert Graham (known as 'Bumper' Graham) to collect her, on the pretext that a UDA commander wanted to see her. Graham lost patience while waiting for her and went into the building to fetch her out.

The full savagery of the beating became clear as the arrested women, impressed by how much the police already seemed to know, gave the full story. Ann Ogilby had been led upstairs, followed by three masked women. She was seated on the bench and blindfolded and the sack placed over her head. Her assailants were three teenage girls, Etta Cowan and Christine Smith (both only sixteen) and Joey Brown. According to their own testimony, they punched, beat and kicked their victim, then began to beat her on the head with bricks. Graham and Joey Brown, realising that the attack had gone far beyond even conventional brutality, tried to stop it, but the other two attackers refused. At this point, Ann Ogilby's daugher had returned, and they heard her knock and call for her mother. Graham and Brown went out of the room, and he then drove Sharlene to the YWCA hostel. Cowan and Smith paused for a cigarette before resuming their assault. By this time, Ann Ogilby had collapsed and when Etta Cowan removed the sack they realized that she was dead. They stuffed the body into another sack, carried it to the ground floor and left it there while they went to report to Elizabeth Douglas. Eventually, probably by men of the UDA, the body was moved out and dumped by the motorway.

In February 1975, eleven women and one man ('Bumper' Graham) were put on trial for the murder of Ann Ogilby. All pleaded guilty. Cowan and Smith were convicted of murder, and sentenced to be detained 'at the pleasure of the Secretary of State' – the legal phrase for the long-term imprisonment of a minor. Elizabeth Douglas pleaded guilty to manslaughter and received a ten-year sentence. Graham and Brown were convicted of causing grievous bodily harm;

they and all the other accused were sent to prison, apart from one sixteen-year-old girl, convicted of intimidation, who received a suspended sentence. The judge, Lord Justice McGonigle, commented on 'a vicious and brutalising organisation of persons who take the law into their own hands, and who, by kangaroo courts and the infliction of physical brutality, terrorize a neighbourhood through intimidation.'

Such was the power and terror wielded by Elizabeth Douglas and her 'heavy mob' or punishment squad, that at no point had Ann Ogilby dared to complain, seek help or resist, though the true reason for Graham's arrival at the Social Services centre must have been all too obvious to her.

MR HALL AND MR BALL

The names Mr Hall and Mr Ball have a faintly ridiculous ring to them, as if they were some obscure comedians or a forgotten music hall act. In reality, they were amongst the aliases of the sex-murderers Geoffrey Evans and John Shaw, who vowed that they would murder a woman a week, and were about to abduct their third victim when the Gardai apprehended them. It is fortunate that serial killers rarely operate in pairs, for they seem to encourage each other in a spiralling trail of ever more brutal outrages. Evans and Shaw, like the Hillside Stranglers, killed their victims to escape being identified afterwards. In another country, they might have avoided capture for longer, but Ireland is a small place and they were tracked down in a few weeks. It was just as well, for had their spree continued they would have killed and killed again.

Geoffrey Evans and John Shaw were small-time English criminals, with a long record of convictions for offences like indecent assault, burglary and theft. Evans was the dominant member of the pair; he planned the kidnappings and selected the victims, usually preferring small women. The physically imposing John Shaw was his pliable accomplice, who provided the muscle to bully and intimidate their prisoners. He also killed the victims when Evans ordered him to.

The two men arrived in Ireland in 1974, after escaping from England where they were wanted by the police for at least three rapes. They are not known to have killed any women up to this point, but they were on the run because their last victim had recognized them. In future, Evans and Shaw decided, they would kill any woman who fell into their clutches.

On arriving in Ireland, the two criminals travelled to Fethard, County Tipperary, where they had a friend in the town. They embarked on a spree of housebreakings and thefts, which led to their arrest and imprisonment in early 1975. After serving eighteen months, the two thugs were released within a few weeks of each other in August 1976. They returned to Fethard and borrowed a car from their friend, then drove off to Dublin, where they collected a suit-case belonging to Evans. Afterwards they headed to Brittas Bay, a popular summer resort about thirty miles south of the city. They were attracted by the large number of holi-day caravans around the strand, which they thought would provide rich pickings for burglars at this time of the year.

Evans had more in mind than mere theft. Whilst drinking in Jack White's pub a few miles from Brittas Bay – where almost twenty years later an unknown assassin was to gun down the publican, Tom Nevin – he suggested they kidnap a young woman and rape her. They left the pub and drove around to find an isolated hideaway in which they could carry out the crime, and then began looking for a suitable victim. After failing to lure a girl they saw on the roadside into their car, the pair carried on to Jack McDaniel's pub at Brittas Bay, which was full of holidaymakers. They noticed a good-looking young woman named Elizabeth Plunkett amongst the crowd, who was sitting with a group of friends. The attractive Dubliner was with her boyfriend, and on any other night would have stayed in his company and eluded the two criminals. But by the cruellest of coincidences she was about to walk out of the premises alone. Earlier, two members of the group had started an argument about the sale of a car. When the young woman's efforts to stop the bickering were ignored, she became exasperated and decided to go home by herself. Evans and Shaw observed her leaving, and followed their target out of the pub. A trivial quarrel had presented them with their first known murder victim.

In 1976, women in Ireland were not as wary about hitchhiking or accepting lifts as they are today. Nonetheless, Evans dropped Shaw further along the road, before doubling back and stopping to offer Elizabeth Plunkett a lift. After the unsuspecting woman got into the car, he picked up Shaw and they drove on towards Dublin. At Timon Wood, a few miles from Brittas Bay, they stopped the car and pounced on their victim. They carried her into the forest, dragging a heavy suitcase behind them. Shaw was struggling to subdue the young woman, and failed to notice one of her distinctive sandals fall off by the roadside. Inside the wood, they tore off her clothes, and raped her repeatedly. After a while, Evans realized they had left the car in full view on the roadside, and directed his henchman to take it to a car park. Shaw returned after two hours, and they again attacked the brutalized woman. As daybreak approached, Evans told Shaw to kill their captive. His accomplice went to the suitcase and took out a nylon shirt. He went up to the half-conscious Miss Plunkett and choked her to death with it.

Next morning, the two killers left the body concealed in the wood, and returned to Brittas Bay. They robbed a number of caravans, and took note of a rowing boat beside an empty caravan. After dark, they placed their victim in the boot of the car, and drove back to Brittas Bay. They weighted her body down with a stolen lawnmower and put her in the boat. Shaw rowed about thirty yards out to sea and threw

Elizabeth Plunkett overboard. The killers, confident they had not been seen, set up camp nearby. But the next morning, as they were burning the victim's clothes, a patrol car appeared and two Gardai began questioning them. There had been a complaint that the two men were trespassing on private property. Evans and Shaw had taken the precaution of preparing aliases, and replied they were stepbrothers named Murphy. They had jobs in Fethard, and were taking a few days off on a camping holiday.

Since their only crime was trespassing, the officers left after telling them to move on. Evans and Shaw breathed a sigh of relief, and headed back to their base in Fethard. They were lucky that Elizabeth Plunkett had not been reported missing, in which case their goose would have been cooked. Elizabeth's friends assumed she was back in Dublin, and only found she had not returned several days later. Evans and Shaw were aware the police would eventually find out a woman was missing, and probably connect it to the two strange men camping on the beach at Brittas Bay. It was time to keep one step ahead of the law by moving to another part of Ireland. The two men left Fethard and headed for the city of Galway. They had amassed a large sum of cash through their sporadic petty thefts, and used it to buy a caravan in Barna on the outskirts of the city.

They changed their identities, and obtained provisional driving licenses in the false names of Hall and Ball. They stole a car in Clifden, about fifty miles north of Galway City, and roughly painted it black. Once they had given it false number plates they were ready to go hunting for their next victim.

In Brittas Bay, meanwhile, the Gardai had been informed that Elizabeth Plunkett had vanished whilst on holiday in the resort. A major search of the area was set in motion, but it was a week before an officer found the victim's sandal at the entrance of Timon Wood. There was another clue further into the forest. Evans, who had been practising his alias, left a piece of cardboard behind with the name 'Geoffrey Murphy' on it. The Gardai now had a link between the men on the private beach and Elizabeth Plunkett, who they now believed to be dead. Every police officer in the country was told to keep an eye out for the suspected murderers, and their descriptions were published in the national newspapers.

Tragically the alert came a few days too late to prevent Evans and Shaw from killing again. The next murder was even viler than the first, and ranks as one of the most horrific Ireland has ever known. Before the killers set out on their next foray, they scouted out a remote location in the Galway region where they could bring the victim. Evans settled on a small forestry plantation in the grounds of the deserted railway station at Ballinahinch, County Mayo; the body could be dumped in Lough Inagh, which was close by.

On 22 September, Mr Hall and Mr Ball, as they now called themselves, drove north into the beautiful scenic area of Connemara. About twenty miles north of Galway, in the town of Oranmore, they picked up a young hitchhiker. She got into the car, but after a few miles found herself becoming uneasy, although there was nothing overtly threatening in the behaviour of the two men. She asked them to stop at a pub because she wanted to go to the lavatory, and slipped out through the back window. This action probably saved her life. The killers realized she had escaped and continued on their way.

Later that evening, Evans and Shaw stopped at the tiny village of Maam to buy some provisions at a grocery shop.

The owner noticed the crude paint job on their black Ford Cortina, and had the presence of mind to jot down the registration number. The next morning, he read in the newspaper that the police were looking for two Englishmen, and he immediately telephoned his local Garda officer. The car and its occupants became the focus of a nationwide manhunt, but by then the rapists had struck again. At about 11.30 p.m. on 22 September, Evans and Shaw were cruising the streets of Castlebar when they observed a twenty-four-year-old restaurant worker named Mary Duffy in a phone kiosk. She had just rung her brother to tell him she intended walking home, because she could not get a lift from anybody. The killers parked the car up the road and waited till she left the phone box. As she walked past the car, Shaw leapt out and attempted to drag her into the back seat. Mary Duffy had a chronic back problem, but it did not stop her putting up a tremendous fight, and Shaw had to beat her repeatedly around the head to subdue her. During the course of the struggle, he knocked out the young woman's partial denture plate, which was left on the pavement. Eventually, with the help of Evans, Shaw got her into the Ford Cortina and they roared off into the night. Several people in the vicinity heard screams, but assumed it was only teenagers returning home from the pub. The one householder who looked out of his window saw nothing more than a black car pulling away.

On the long drive to Ballinahinch, the kidnappers amused themselves by taking turns to rape their captive in the back seat. When they finally reached the wood beside the railway station, Mary Duffy was tied to a tree while her captors set up a tent. Evans and Shaw sexually assaulted Mary Duffy throughout the night and the following day. In was not until the early hours of 24 September that they put an end the young Mayo woman's agony, when Shaw took a cushion from the car and suffocated her. The killers followed their prearranged plan and dumped her body in Lough Inagh. The next day, they threw their tent and camping equipment in another river, and drove back to their caravan at Barna. Once again, they thought they had hidden their tracks well, and were safe from detection by the police.

It was almost two full days before Mary Duffy's family notified the Gardai that she was missing. A search in Castlebar soon turned up the broken pieces of her false teeth. The detectives investigating the case noted the close parallels with the disappearance of Elizabeth Plunkett. They realized they were seeking two extremely dangerous men, and redoubled their efforts to find the black Cortina. On the evening of September 26, a patrol car in Salthill, the seaside town on the edge of Galway city, came upon the wanted vehicle parked in a side street. The officers called for back-up, and one of them ran off to get help from a nearby Garda station. Evans and Shaw returned a few minutes later, and nearly got away from the one Garda who was on the scene. Fortunately his colleague returned a few seconds later with more officers, and the two men were surrounded. They did not resist arrest and were taken into custody. Afterwards, the Gardai discovered their patrolmen had just prevented another murder. Shaw and Evans, just two days after the murder of Mary Duffy, had targeted another young woman. They were collecting their car so they could follow her.

The two criminals were confined in separate rooms and questioned overnight. The next morning, Shaw tried to escape by wriggling through a toilet window, but was pursued and recaptured within a few minutes. The interrogation continued throughout that day and into the next, but Evans and Shaw would admit nothing. The greatest concern was for Mary Duffy, whom the Gardai thought might still be alive. By the early hours of 28 September, the detectives investigating the case were close to despair at the two men's refusal to cooperate with them. They decided to halt the interviews for a rest, and a young detective was detailed to stay overnight in the police station with the suspects. He could not sleep, and decided to make a further effort to get one of the men to talk. The detective remembered that Shaw, who was showing the strain of his arrest more than Evans, had earlier mentioned he was a Catholic. He woke the suspect up and brought him to the interview room, where he tried to appeal to the kidnapper's better nature. After outlining the anguish the relatives of the missing women were going through, the policeman recited the rosary and asked Shaw to pray with him. The suspect broke down and confessed he had murdered Elizabeth Plunkett and Mary Duffy. The next morning, he gave a full account of the crimes and signed a statement. Evans, when confronted with his friend's confession, reacted by giving his own version of events.

It now remained to find the bodies of the two victims. The remains of Elizabeth Plunkett were washed ashore sixty-five miles south of Brittas Bay shortly afterwards, but it took several weeks to retrieve Mary Duffy from the dark waters of Lough Inagh. Her body was finally recovered on 10 October 1976, when police divers found it trapped in a small cave on the bed of the lake. Lough Inagh has a very high peat content, and the victim's body was almost perfectly preserved, although it had been submerged under twenty-five feet of water for several weeks.

John Shaw was convicted of the murder, rape and unlawful imprisonment of both women, and sentenced to life imprisonment. The judge at Geoffrey Evans' trial directed that he be acquitted of the murder of Elizabeth Plunkett, but he was found guilty of murdering Mary Duffy and of two counts of rape. The defence lawyers appealed the convictions, on the grounds that the Gardai kept Shaw and Evans in custody longer than the forty-eight hours permitted under the Offences Against the State Act. The Supreme Court dismissed the appeal because the police had believed that Mary Duffy might still be alive when they ignored the time limit. The judges ruled that her right of life took precedence over the prisoners' right of liberty. At the time of writing, Evans and Shaw have been in prison for over thirty years, and are Ireland's longest- serving convicts.

SHOOTOUT AT SHANNON CROSS

Before the beginning of the troubles in Northern Ireland, around 1970, policemen in the Republic of Ireland did not expect to be shot at or murdered. But since then, a fair number of Irish Gardai have been shot whilst tackling paramilitary terrorists. On 7 July 1980, one of the most serious incidents of this type took place at Ballaghadereen, County Roscommon. On that day, three armed and masked raiders entered the Bank of Ireland in that town, and held up the staff and customers. They fired a number of shots, and threatened two local Gardai, but fortunately nobody was injured. They left the bank with over £45,000 and sped off in a white Ford Cortina car.

The Gardai in the surrounding towns were alerted, and a car was sent out from Castlerea Station to intercept the gang. It contained three uniformed officers – Sergeant M. O'Malley and Gardai Henry Byrne and Glen O'Kelly – and Detective Garda John Morley. The only armed policeman was Detective Morley, who was carrying an Israeli-made Uzi submachine gun. The police car sped towards a cross-roads called Shannon Cross, hoping to block the gang's escape route. As they approached the intersection, the Ford Cortina came hurtling towards them from another direction. The two vehicles collided and came to a halt. One of the armed robbers leapt out with a rifle, and began shooting through the windscreen of the patrol car. Miraculously, his bullets missed the two officers in the front of the car, but Garda Byrne, sitting in the back seat, was hit and died instantly. The bank robbers reversed their damaged car and drove off, with Gardai Morley and O'Kelly in pursuit on foot. A little distance down the road, they abandoned the car, leaving the proceeds of the robbery in the boot, and took to the fields. Detective Morley, still on the road, fired a burst from his Uzi at the running men. One of them turned and fired back, hitting the officer, who fell to the ground mortally wounded. The fleeing bank robbers split up and escaped.

In the aftermath of the robbery, the Gardai saturated the area with officers, since there was a good chance the bank robbers would not be able to get far on foot. The first fugitive was found quite quickly in a wood about ten miles from Shannon Cross. He had been shot in the chest and was badly wounded. He gave his name as O'Shea, but refused to cooperate any further with his captors. The prisoner was placed under an armed guard and taken to hospital. Chief Superintendent John Courtney of the murder squad, who was in charge of the operation, now instituted a grid search of the surrounding countryside. On 9 January, the second of the three men was captured in fields near French Park, County Roscommon. He was later identified as Patrick McCann. The third bank robber evaded capture, and was found to have got away in a hijacked lorry. His two accomplices would not identify him, but the Gardai received information that he was a man named Peter Pringle. Chief Superintendent Courtney believed he was hiding out in Galway, and placed a watch on his girlfriend. On 19 July, she was followed to a house outside of the city, where Pringle was staying. Armed Gardai moved in and arrested him.

The three men were tried for the murder of Garda Byrne in

November 1980. They were judged in the Special Criminal Court, which dealt with political and terrorist offences and did not have a jury. The evidence against the three men included the counter of the bank at Ballaghadereen, which had O'Shea's footprint upon it. Other forensic evidence included fragments of paint and glass from the bullet-riddled patrol car, which were found on O'Shea's clothes. All three of the accused were convicted and sentenced to death. Nobody had been hanged in Ireland for decades, and the sentences were commuted to life imprisonment.

There was some controversy about the conviction of Peter Pringle, who claimed he was not involved in the robbery and murders. An important part of the case against him was a verbal admission of his guilt, which he was alleged to have made to the police at the time of his arrest. He denied ever making this statement, and he refused to sign a written confession whilst in custody. In 1995, the Court of Criminal Appeal, following new evidence that cast doubt upon the case against him, quashed Mr Pringle's conviction.

THE GERMAN CONSUL

At the height of the troubles in Northern Ireland, cases of murder by mistake were frequent. Either a victim was wrongly identified, or something went wrong during 'operations', and a violent death which had not been intended nevertheless happened. Such cases give an added edge of tragedy to what is always a terrible event – the taking of another person's life. One of the most widely publicized of such 'accidents' was the killing of Thomas Niedermayer, a respected German businessman and the managing director of the Grundig electronics factory at Dunmurry. Niedermayer lived in Belfast with his wife and two daughters and had no connections of any sort either with Republican or Unionist politics or factions.

Niedermayer's evil fortune was to be a resident of a small luxury estate, Glengoland Gardens, just on the edge of the Andersonstown district of Belfast. It is believed that he may once have been stopped by a Provisional IRA group, seeking to hijack a car, and dissuaded them by showing them papers establishing his foreign nationality. In addition, he had diplomatic status as the honorary West German consul in Belfast. But from then on, the Provisionals knew that an important foreign citizen lived conveniently close to one of their own strongholds.

Thomas Niedermayer's name came up again in their discussions in December 1973. Nine IRA members had been convicted of bomb attacks in London, and were sentenced to life or long-term imprisonment in mid-November of that year. Two of those sentenced to life, Marion and Dolores Price, went on hunger-strike in order to draw attention to their claim to serve their sentences in Northern Ireland rather than in British gaols. Their hunger-strike attracted international attention. The British authorities refused the sisters' claim and had them force-fed. To put additional pressure on the British government, the Provisional IRA decided to organize a kidnapping. In effect, they would demand the transfer of the Price sisters in return for the freedom of the kidnapped person. In order for this to be successful, someone of high status had to be found as their kidnap victim. Niedermayer seemed the ideal person, since his kidnapping would not only severely embarrass the British government, but would also bring strong pressure from West Germany to obtain his release.

The date for the kidnapping was set as 27 December. Niedermayer's wife was in hospital, and he had visited her that evening. Just after 10.45 p.m., the doorbell rang. It was answered by his daughter Renate, who found two men on the doorstep. They said they had crashed into Niedermayer's car, which was parked on the street. Niedermayer came out, still in carpet slippers, to look. They examined the German's Ford Granada car, then, as Niedermayer returned towards his house, the men grabbed him and forced him into their own car, which had been waiting with engine running and a man at the wheel. They disappeared into the night. The abduction had been witnessed from across the road by Niedermayer's neighbour and colleague in the Grundig works, another German, Herbert Hoech, who had been alerted by the sound of the car engine. At first. he supposed some prank was going on, but after telephoning the Niedermayer house and speaking to Renate, he called the police.

Nothing more was heard. No public ransom demand was ever submitted. No one claimed responsibility for the kidnapping of Thomas Niedermayer. There was widespread sympathy for his family. Church leaders united in asking for anyone who could give information to do so, saying: 'Amidst so much suffering and tragedy in Ireland at the present time the disappearance of the German consul constitutes an altogether special case.' Gradually, a little information began to leak out. The Provisional IRA had sent a message to the British government, soon after the kidnapping, stating that Niedermayer would be killed unless the Price sisters were moved to Northern Ireland. The British government had refused any negotiation, and the RUC had not been informed about the message.

This information was established by the Democratic Unionist politician, the Reverend Ian Paisley, whose criticism of the British government was shared by many not in his party. The detectives who had been painstakingly following up every possible lead felt severely let down. Meanwhile there was still no indication of Niedermayer's fate. The hunger strike went on into June and then came to an end (the Price sisters were ultimately moved to Armagh Prison a year later). Any hopes in his family for the German consul's release following this were dashed. The silence continued.

It was seven years later, in March 1980, that a man's skeletal remains, with pieces of clothing, were found by the driver of an excavator clearing a dump at Colin Glen, on the west side of Belfast and not far from Andersonstown. The police were called immediately, and the remains carefully examined and removed. In charge of the case was

Detective-Inspector Alan Simpson, who subsequently wrote a book about this and other investigations. His team were already virtually certain that the body was that of Herr Niedermayer, but it remained to be proved. Forensic investigation showed that the skull was indented in a way compatible with blows on the head from a pistol butt. Although these blows might not have been sufficient to cause death, it was clear from them and from the way the legs had been tied, that the man had not died a natural death. Frau Ingeborg Niedermayer, who was still living in Belfast, was able to confirm the fragments of clothing as corresponding with her husband's. In the end, as often with fragmentary remains, it was the dead man's teeth and his dental records that proved conclusive in establishing who he was.

A massive police operation to gather information now went into action. With international (and especially German) interest in the case again at full height, the Belfast CID were on their mettle to show results. Despite the complete lack of progress made by the police in the initial investigations, now, seven years on, a number of productive leads were opened up and pursued, undoubtedly through the cooperation of informers and undercover agents. Some four weeks after the positive identification of the body, an early morning combined police–military operation pulled in four people for questioning. One was the woman who had been living in the house now known to be where the victim was held, in Hillhead Crescent, Andersonstown; a second was the owner of the Ford Cortina car which had been 'borrowed' for use in the kidnap. The two others were Eugene McManus, identified as adjutant of the Belfast Brigade of the Provisional IRA at the time; and John Bradley, identified as a training officer of the first battalion of the Provisional IRA. Interrogated at Castlereagh Detention Centre, the four yielded information which enabled the story of Thomas Niedermayer's kidnapping and death to be told.

Approved by the IRA high command in Dublin, the kidnapping was organized in Andersonstown. On Boxing Day, 1973, the house was selected and its occupant told to vacate it for a few days. The following day the car was 'borrowed' from its owner in an Andersonstown drinking club. The kidnap went off according to plan, and Niedermayer was confined in an upstairs room in the house in Hillhead Crescent. Perhaps confident at first that he would be quickly released, he remained calm and tried to engage his captors in conversation, but they had been instructed not to talk to him. By the third day of his imprisonment, Niedermayer was beginning to become agitated. On the excuse of going to the lavatory, he tried to escape but was restrained by his four guards, who included Bradley. The prisoner struggled and shouted for help, at one point getting close to a window. The guards forced him back onto the mattress and tried to gag him and tie his legs. As the struggle continued, someone hit Niedermayer several times on the head with the butt of an automatic pistol. The four men piled on top of him, pressing his face into the mattress. Eventually the prisoner's body went completely still, and they realized that he was dead. Most of this testimony came from Bradley, with McManus confirming the broader picture. The operation had gone disastrously wrong. Instead of a high-profile kidnap victim, the Provisionals had a corpse. A damage-limitation exercise was rapidly put into action. Under instructions, the team of guards arranged for the room in which Niedermayer had been held and murdered to be completely redecorated, the mattress disposed of and a new bed supplied. They picked the dump-site at Colin Glen and under cover of darkness dug a shallow grave. The body was brought out in the boot of a car, and dropped in face-first. According to Bradley, the four said a prayer over the grave, before dragging an old mattress over it. Had it not been for a council decision to clear the dump-site and restore Colin Glen to its former attractiveness, the body might never have been found. The Provisional IRA clamped an order of silence over the affair. Nothing was said, no responsibility was claimed.

The only two people to stand trial were Bradley and McManus, the former on a charge of false imprisonment and murder, and of membership of the Provisional IRA; the second on the ultimately reduced charges of withholding information, impeding the work of the police, and member-ship of the Provisional IRA. In the case of others, known or suspected to have been involved, some of whom were already in prison, the police were unable to find sufficient evidence for commitment to trial or, as in the case of the house and car owners, accepted coercion as a reason for their complicity and silence, and did not press charges. The trial took place in February 1981, before Lord Justice Jones. Bradley pleaded guilty to the reduced charge of manslaughter and was sentenced to twenty years imprison-ment. McManus pleaded guilty as charged and was given five years.

The Niedermayer case, because of the involvement of a foreign citizen, because of the bungled handling by the kidnappers, because of the failure of the forces of justice to bring all the killers to account, and because of the British government's refusal to pass information on to its own Northern Irish police force, remains a shabby episode from a dreadful period. It had a tragic sequel in the suicide by drowning of Niedermayer's wife, Ingeborg, a few years after the burial of her murdered husband's remains.

THE STRANGE CASE OF MALCOLM McARTHUR

Some readers of this book may be familiar with the slang word 'gubu', which is used to describe an embarrassing foul-up. Not many, however, will know how it originated. Like the American word 'snafu', which has a similar meaning, gubu is an acronym. It is formed out of the first letters of Grotesque, Unbelievable, Bizarre and Unprecedented. Gubu was coined in 1982 by the journalist and writer, Conor Cruise O'Brien, after hearing Charles Haughey, the Taoiseach (Prime Minister) of Ireland use these words to describe a remarkable double murder case. The arrest of Malcolm McArthur, the man wanted for these crimes, embarrassed the government and reverberated into the highest circles of the land. Even today, many journalists who followed the case believe there was a political cover-up, and that the trial was manipulated to avoid revealing all the facts. McArthur's violent rampage inspired John Banville to write the novel The Book of Evidence, a classic psychological study of the mind of a murderer.

On the face of it, Malcolm McArthur was as unlikely a killer as ever took another human life. He came from a privileged background, and was the son of a wealthy County Meath farmer. The quiet young man was well educated, and most of his acquaintances assumed he was an academic, or a scientist of some sort. This view was reinforced by his taste for cravats, bow ties and tweed jackets, all of which gave him a rather donnish appearance. In the 1970s, McArthur settled in Dublin, where his comfortable lifestyle was paid for from his extensive private means. He had received £76,000 in 1976 following the death of his father, and a further £10,000 more from his mother in 1980.

This was a large nest egg by any standards and should have left him financially comfortable. Yet he was a big spender, and had no income from regular employment. By the summer of 1982, McArthur, who had moved with his girlfriend and young son to Tenerife, was almost broke. Like many before him, he was discovering that 'it is easier to spend a sovereign than earn a penny'. Eventually he hit on what he considered to be a sure-fire method to replenish his depleted funds. There was plenty of money in Ireland – he would go home and steal some of it. He arranged to return home and put his scheme into operation.

The fact that he lacked any criminal experience did not deter McArthur. In July 1982, he flew back into Dublin and booked into a guesthouse in Dun Laoghaire, six miles south of the city. The would-be gangster's first priority was the acquisition of a firearm. He started going to clay pigeon shooting competitions, hoping he would be able to steal an unattended shotgun. But his suspicious behaviour at one of these events nearly led to his arrest, and he instead began looking for one in the sales columns of the national newspapers. His second requirement was a getaway vehicle. On the exceptionally warm afternoon of 22 July 1982, he went to Phoenix Park in Dublin, where he planned to steal a car.

McArthur had grown a beard, and was wearing spectacles and a woollen hat. He had also put a heavy sweater over his open shirt, despite the boiling hot weather. The prospective car thief was carrying a large canvas holdall, which contained an imitation wooden pistol, a spade and a heavy claw hammer. He wandered around the park for a while, and eventually noticed a woman sunbathing in the grass beside her car, a silver Renault 5. McArthur sneaked up from behind and held her up with his imitation pistol. His victim, a nurse named Bridie Gargan, had stopped to enjoy the sun on her way home from St James's Hospital, where she had just finished a shift. She thought he was joking at first, but after a moment obeyed his order to get into the back seat of the car. Suddenly the nurse realized that McArthur planned to take her as well as the vehicle, and began to panic. Without hesitation her kidnapper took out the hammer and gave her two heavy blows on the head. She slumped onto the back seat, blood pouring from her shattered skull.

A gardener at the nearby US Ambassador's residence had seen McArthur, and bravely ran up to apprehend the car thief. McArthur held him off with his fake gun, then leapt into the vehicle and drove off at high speed, leaving his spade behind him. The gardener ran off to alert the Gardai, but, before a patrol car could intervene, McArthur had a piece of luck. An ambulance driver, stopped beside the Renault 5 at an intersection and noticed there was an injured woman on the back seat. On seeing Bridie Gargan's Hospital Staff sticker on the windscreen, he assumed McArthur was a doctor with an accident victim. The driver turned on his siren and gestured to the car to follow behind. Within minutes, the speeding ambulance had led McArthur through the heavy rush hour traffic, and he was pulling into the grounds of St James's Hospital. The ambulance went on its way, leaving McArthur to turn round and drive back out. He parked the car nearby and ran off, leaving his bloodstained victim on the back seat. Bridie Gargan had suffered mortal head wounds and was in a coma; she died four days later without gaining consciousness.

After abandoning the car, McArthur attempted to cover his tracks before going home to the guesthouse in Dun Laoghaire. He took a bus to Ballymun, on the northside of Dublin, where he walked into a pub and shaved off his beard before ordering a taxi. The next day, when the attack on Nurse Gargan was the lead story in every Irish newspaper, a taxi-driver confirmed he had picked up a man from the pub and brought him to Dun Laoghaire. The Gardai began asking shopkeepers in the town if they had noticed anybody fitting McArthur's description recently.

The man they were seeking soon killed again, and the second murder was as brutal and meaningless as the first. Two days after his assault on Bridie Gargan, McArthur hitched a lift out to Edenderry, County Offaly, where he had arranged to meet Donal Dunne, a local farmer selling a double-barrelled Spanish shotgun. Dunne met McArthur in the town, and they drove out on the Rathdangan road in his car to try out the weapon. Dunne stopped at a bog a few miles along the way, and handed the loaded weapon to McArthur, who said he was sorry, then turned the gun on the farmer and shot him in the face, killing him instantly. The murderer got into the dead man's car and headed for Dublin, where he parked the vehicle in a side street in the city centre. McArthur was observed by the people in another Offaly vehicle that was following him, under the impression he would lead them to Croke Park, where the county team were playing in a hurling match that afternoon. The

Gaelic Sports fans' description of the car driver helped the Gardai establish a connection between the Donal Dunne and Bridie Gargan cases.

The body of Donal Dunne was discovered on the following day, when a family stopped at the murder site to pick raspberries. One of the children saw a hand peeping from under a cardboard box that McArthur had used to conceal the body, and told his father, who raised the alarm. The murder squad soon confirmed their belief that the same man had committed the murders of Bridie Gargan and Donal Dunne. Fingerprints taken from the shovel at the murder scene in Phoenix Park were matched with those on a newspaper and milk carton found in Edenderry, at the place where Donal Dunne picked up his killer.

On 4 August, McArthur suddenly appeared at the door of a retired American diplomat, who lived in the affluent village of Killiney, County Dublin. The American did not recognize his caller, but, when the stranger mentioned he had been at several parties in the house, invited him in. Once inside McArthur produced a shotgun, and demanded a large sum of money, which the diplomat did not have in the house. Shortly afterwards, he distracted McArthur's attention, and managed to slip out and make his escape. The diplomat phoned the Gardai, but by the time they arrived the intruder was gone. The failed robbery had a peculiar aftermath. It can only be guessed that McArthur thought he had been recognized, since the next day he rang the diplomat and apologized for his regrettable 'practical joke'. McArthur then offered to ring the local police station and clear up the matter, which he did shortly afterwards. He named himself to the police officer who answered the call as Malcolm McArthur, and told his unlikely story of a prank that had gone wrong. The information was passed on to Chief Superintendent John Courtney, who was leading the investigation into the Gargan and Dunne murders. The Gardai in Dun Laoghaire were already following up a report by a local news vendor. One of his regular customers had recently shaved his beard off and fitted the description of the suspect they were hunting. The vendor also mentioned that the man usually wore a cravat. Chief Superintendent Courtney was sure they were on the track of the double killer, and believed he was still in the area. But suddenly the trail went cold; either the suspect had escaped altogether or he was laying low somewhere.

In fact, McArthur had taken refuge in Dalkey about two miles south of Dun Laoghaire. He had chosen a hideout that was so unbelievable no writer would dare introduce it into a novel or screenplay. The most wanted man in Ireland was staying in a flat belonging to the Attorney General, Patrick Cassidy. The overall head of the police force and the judiciary had been a friend of McArthur's for several years. The two men had originally met through McArthur's girlfriend, and since then Cassidy had taken a paternal interest in the young couple. The Attorney General, who had no knowledge of his old acquaintance's recent violent exploits, was delighted to see him when he called at his flat on the evening of 4 August. He had a message from McArthur's girlfriend, who had phoned because she was worried about McArthur's whereabouts.

Cassidy invited McArthur to stay in the flat as his guest, and the killer made himself at home. Over the next few days he stayed out of sight, and ordered his newspapers and groceries to be delivered by taxi. McArthur had yet to steal a penny, and he did not intend abandoning his criminal activities before acquiring the money he needed to stay in Tenerife. Notes and diagrams later found in the apartment revealed he had several plans in mind, including the murder of an unspecified female relative. McArthur's rare forays into the outside world were made with the Attorney General in his chauffeur-driven government limousine. On Sunday, the two men went to watch the All-Ireland semi-final at Croke Park, where McArthur sat in the VIP box with a number of leading politicians; a few seats away, his host was being updated on the search for the double murderer by the Garda Commissioner, Ireland's top policeman.

The Gardai were searching high and low for the wanted man, and it was inevitable they would eventually catch up with him. On Thursday 12 August, a detective making door-to-door inquiries visited the block of flats, and one of the tenants recognized the description of McArthur as the man staying with the Attorney General. Chief Superintendent Courtney spoke to one of their mutual friends, and confirmed that Patrick Cassidy was close to the wanted man. Courtney now had a difficult decision on his hands. In normal circumstances, he would have gone to the apartment and arrested McArthur without warning, but the Attorney General was an important public representative. Should he inform Mr Cassidy in advance of the raid on his home? Chief Superintendent Courtney decided there would be no exception to normal police procedure. He was convinced his officers had found the right man, but if they were wrong he would take responsibility and face the backlash. The Gardai obtained a warrant, and prepared to move in on McArthur.

On the afternoon of Friday 13 August, a squad of armed detectives called at the front door of the block of flats.

McArthur did not answer, but an alert policeman noticed a face peering through one of the flat windows. The suspect had only returned a few minutes earlier, after dumping his imitation gun in a nearby harbour. The officers sealed off the block and waited for the Attorney General to return. Cassidy arrived an hour later and was told his house guest was wanted for armed robbery. He handed over the house keys and the detectives ran in and stormed the flat. There had been fears that McArthur, who was still armed, might put up a fight, but he was found hiding in the bathroom. As the suspect was led away, Cassidy walked over and told him he was 'on his own for this'. McArthur was probably relieved that he had finally been arrested after his murderous spree. He cooperated fully with the police, and signed a full statement on the morning of his arrest, confessing to the murders of Bridie Gargan and Donal Dunne.

The capture of the most wanted man in Ireland in the home of the Attorney General caused uproar in the media, and damaged public confidence in the Fianna Fáil government of the time. The following day, Patrick Cassidy went on a prearranged visit to the United States, but he cut short his stay when news of the arrest broke in the press. He returned to find his position as Attorney General threatened, and resigned a few days later. He was unfortunate, since he had done nothing wrong except put up a friend who had previously been of spotless character. Yet somebody had to take responsibility for the gubu. Very few details of the circumstances surrounding the hunt for McArthur had been released, and the media expected that many of their outstanding questions would be answered at the trial. Journalists were disgusted by what happened next. McArthur was charged with only one of the murders, that of Bridie Gargan, to which he entered a plea of guilty. He was then sentenced to life imprisonment and led away. No evidence of any kind was given, and the whole business was over in a matter of minutes. Such conveyor-belt justice was not uncommon at the time, mainly because Ireland was in a financial crisis and legal expenses were being cut to the bone. But, in this case, it inevitably caused speculation that McArthur had received special treatment because of who, or what, he knew.

THE MONKSTOWN MURDER

Sometimes a murder turns up such contradictory evidence that the culprit eludes detection. The murder of Charles Self was such a case, and every lead the police followed petered out in a dead end. The victim's body was found in the hall of his mews house in the fashionable Dublin suburb of Monkstown, on the morning of Thursday 21 January 1982. Mr Self had been strangled with his own dressing gown cord, and a kitchen knife had been used to cut his throat and inflict multiple stab wounds on his body. The murder weapon, which was one of a set belonging to the dead man, lay on the floor of the living room, which had been ransacked. The killer had left a bloody footprint on the carpet. A downstairs window was wide open, suggesting that the murderer had either entered or left the house by this route. Forensic experts found a number of fingerprints in the downstairs room, which it was hoped might help find the murderer.

A man named Bertie Tryer, who was sharing the house with the deceased, discovered the body. He told the Gardai he had been asleep upstairs, and did not hear the sounds of a fight. But his slumbers were disturbed twice in the night. When Mr Tryer came back to the house the previous evening at around 11 p.m., Charles Self was still out; when the witness went to bed shortly afterwards, Self had still not returned. Around 2 a.m., he was woken by the sound of voices downstairs, but fell back asleep. Some time later, Mr Tryer was disturbed again when a strange man entered his room; the intruder said 'Sorry, wrong bedroom' and left again. He described this man as well spoken, aged about twenty-four, and dressed in jeans and a jacket; he had curly hair and was clean-shaven. Afterwards he had heard or seen nothing else until he came down for breakfast, when he stumbled on the victim's body. An elderly lady, whose house shared the courtyard off Brighton Avenue where the mews was situated, recalled seeing a man who resembled this description on the previous day. He had been staring intently through the gate at Mr Self's house. In the early hours of the morning, she had heard somebody in the court-yard moving a heavy garden bench. The old lady went to the window and saw a shadowy figure climbing over the perimeter wall into the next-door garden.

Her evidence suggested that the murder might have been the result of a burglary that went wrong. Yet there were several reasons to suggest an alternative theory. Nothing appeared to have been stolen from the house, despite the havoc left in the living room.

Moreover the lifestyle of the victim suggested he might easily have brought the killer home with him. Charles Self, a thirty-nine-year-old set designer with RTE (the Irish television service), had enjoyed an exceptionally busy social life. He was also openly homosexual, and was well known in Dublin's thriving gay scene. His friends said that he often brought young men he met in the city centre back to the mews; occasionally these would be male prostitutes. It was possible that a man came home with the set designer on the previous evening, and for some unknown reason attacked and murdered him. The motive might have been robbery, or a quarrel that got out of hand. It was also possible that Mr Self made a mistake and linked up with a heterosexual, or even a serial killer who preyed on homosexuals.

Detectives urgently needed to speak to members of the gay community, so they could trace the murdered man's movements on the night of his death, and find out if he had been seen with anybody. This was more difficult to do than it should have been. In 1980, homosexuality was still illegal in Ireland, and the heavy-handed attitude of some officers was not liable to encourage a spirit of cooperation. The suspicions of homosexuals about the motives of the Gardai were increased when it was reported that detectives had visited the Irish Gay Federation, and demanded to see the organization's membership list. The Gardai denied this accusation, but the controversy did not help their legitimate inquiries into the murder of Mr Self. Nonetheless, many of the dead man's gay friends came forward to help find the killer, and the Gardai were able to piece together his movements. Charles Self had been seen a number of times around Burgh Quay, a favourite meeting place for homosexuals in Dublin. A young man with longish blond hair, who wore a dark suit and pale coloured shirt, accompanied him. The description was confirmed by a taxi-driver who brought the set designer and his companion to Brighton Avenue at about 12.45 a.m. He had last seen them walking up Brighton Avenue in the direction of the mews. The driver said that the young man was very drunk, and had to urinate against a wall as soon as he got out of the taxi.

The police did all in their power to trace this young man, who was an important witness, and may well have murdered Charles Self. They could not find him, which suggests he was not a regular habitué of the gay scene in Dublin. He may have been a visitor to the city, either from abroad or from another part of Ireland; perhaps he was a closet homosexual who rarely went to the city's gay haunts. The failure to find this suspect brought the inquiry to a grinding halt.

It was quite possible that the mysterious guest had killed Charles Self, for one of a variety of reasons – or just as likely for no good reason at all. On the other hand, he might have had nothing to do with the death. Perhaps he spent a pleasant hour or two with the set-designer, and then departed, leaving his host alive and well – to be killed by somebody else later in the night. There are many reasons why the blond young man might not have contacted the police, apart from the obvious one that he was a murderer. If he was a foreigner, he could have left Dublin the following morning without realisng his previous night's partner was dead. He could have been an Irishman with a wife or parents, whom he feared would discover he was secretly a homosexual.

There is one piece of evidence that contradicts the theory that this mystery man murdered Charles Self. It lies in Bertie Tryer's description of the stranger who entered his bedroom in the middle of the night. If his memory was accurate – and it should be said that he only saw the person for a moment – this was not the set designer's blond-haired friend. There was a gap of several hours between Charles Self coming home with the blond man in the suit and the brief appearance of the man wearing jeans in Tryer's bedroom. Did another visitor arrive after the first had left, perhaps somebody with a grudge against Charles Self? Could a burglar have entered through the window to find a dead body in the hall, and the living room already in disarray? Or did the man in the jeans only exist as a false memory in the confused imagination of the drowsy Bertie Tryer? The fictional expertise of an Inspector Morse or Wexford would be needed to unravel such a tangle of theories, with a Colin Dexter or Ruth Rendell providing strategic clues and a few lucky breaks along the way. The real-life Gardai who tried to solve the murder of Charles Self were denied such help, and the identity of the killer remains unknown to this day.

THE KIRWAN STREET MURDER

The unplanned murder, carried out in a sudden moment of anger or lust, often leaves detectives with plenty of evidence, but no suspects. When somebody spontaneously kills another human being, they invariably leave forensic traces like fingerprints or strands of hair at the murder scene. It is not uncommon for the murderer – in his haste to get away – to leave behind his weapon, or a personal possession like a ring or watch. These are invaluable clues, and help link the perpetrator to his or her crime. On the other hand, the random murderer is difficult to track down, since there is nothing to connect him to his victim. In many cases, the police do not even know in what general area to start looking for a suspect, especially if the victim is killed in the centre of a city like Dublin, which is ringed by densely populated suburbs. The murderer, even if he has left telling evidence behind him, can be as hard to find as a single marked grain in a field of wheat.

It is important to preserve the crime scene when investigating these casual murders, since a small and seemingly irrelevant object might be the only key to tracing the killer. The Gardai in the Denise Flanagan case nearly lost their most significant clue at the outset of the investigation. As two ambulance men arrived to examine her body for signs of life, they nearly stepped on a pair of spectacles lying in the dirt a few yards away. Fortunately an observant security guard, who was keeping the crowd of onlookers away from the body, warned them to watch where they put their feet. It was just as well that he did, since without these humble glasses the crime would probably have remained unsolved.

The body of Denise Flanagan, a hospital worker, was found on the morning of 25 September 1983, in a lane off Kirwan Street in Dublin, only a few hundred yards from where she lived. She had been throttled during the course of a particularly savage attack, and her clothing and accessories lay scattered around the alley. Her killer had left bite marks on her upper body. If these could be matched to the teeth that inflicted them the results would be invaluable evidence at a trial, although the technique had yet to be tried in Ireland. The proximity of the spectacles to the victim's body left no doubt they belonged to the murderer; he had probably dropped them whilst grappling with her. The frames were a popular brand sold in large quantities by Irish opticians, while the slightly tinted lenses were equally common.

The Gardai quickly traced Miss Flanagan's movements on the night of the murder. She had gone out dancing with a group of her workmates, and visited several nightclubs around the city. She left the last one alone, and was next seen in a fast-food restaurant in O'Connell Street, in the company of an unidentified young man. The witness saw her on the street about ten minutes later, where she was getting into a cab with the same man. A taxi-driver contacted the Gardai and told them he remembered driving a man and a woman to Manor Street, a short walk from the laneway where Miss Flanagan was murdered. The couple had been necking in the back seat. When he reached Manor Street, the young man followed his female companion out of the cab. The driver recalled that Miss Flanagan asked him 'Are you not staying on?' confirming his impression that the second passenger had originally planned to go to another destination.

Both of the witnesses stated the man had not been wearing glasses, but this was irrelevant because he might have removed them for some reason. Chief Superintendent John Courtney, the murder squad detective in charge of the investigation, decided to look for the optician who had supplied the pair at the murder scene. This became a massive logistics exercise for the detectives who undertook the task, since almost every optician in Ireland stocked the brand. The police visited hundreds of premises in Dublin and its suburbs during the search, and checked nearly 250,000 prescriptions for eyeglasses. Luckily the spectacles were fairly new, and the investigators were spared the impossible job of checking old records. After two weeks, a detective in the dormitory suburb of Blanchardstown found the man who had made them. An optician in the village recalled he had recently supplied a pair of glasses fitting this description to Michael Flynn, a twenty-four-year-old local man. The Gardai went to his home and brought him in for an interview with Chief Superintendent John Courtney.

Michael Flynn closely resembled the descriptions of the man seen with Denise Flanagan, and he was unable to give an alibi for the time of the murder. As the interview progressed he became agitated, and soon confessed to the senseless murder of the young woman. He explained that after getting out of the cab, he walked the victim into Kirwan Street, where they stopped and began kissing and cuddling. The couple then went up the lane to continue their petting session in some privacy, but Miss Flanagan objected when he tried to fondle her private parts. Flynn would not stop, and she began struggling, and attempted to get away from him. He lost his self-control and assaulted the young woman, following which he strangled her. He had removed his spectacles earlier in the evening because they kept slipping off his nose, and placed them in his top pocket. It was only when Flynn got home that he realized they were missing, and must have slipped out of his pocket during the assault.

The investigation was notable as it was the first time in Ireland that spectacles and the matching of bite marks with teeth were used to track down a murderer. Michael Flynn pleaded guilty and was sentenced to life imprisonment. In his confession, he described how he felt after the brutal attack. 'I was sick and I hoped that what happened was a dream . . . I was going to go to a police station. I was going to go to confession and I was going to go to the Samaritans but I did not. I was going to commit suicide by jumping in front of a train. I was worried about the effect on my family and I still am.'

THE LOVE RIVALS

In June 1992, a trial took place at Downpatrick which riveted public attention both in Northern Ireland and beyond. Susan Christie, a trainee officer with the Royal Irish Regiment (the former Ulster Defence Regiment) was accused of the murder of Penny McAllister, the wife of a British Army officer. It was the kind of trial which reveals all kinds of intimate details, and the interest of these was heightened by the fact that the accused and the victim's husband, Captain Duncan McAllister of the Royal Signals, were both serving in the British Army. Christie did not deny the killing. Her plea was that she had committed the lesser crime of manslaughter, rather than the premeditated murder with which she had been charged. The murder had been discovered when a family picnicking in Drumkeeragh Forest, in the hills of County Down, were alarmed by the sudden appearance of a young woman, accompanied by two dogs. Her manner was distraught, and her clothes were ripped and bloodstained. 'Help Penny. Go and help Penny – please,' she gasped.

The Rice family, their picnic thus disrupted, took the woman in their car to the nearest town, Ballynahinch, where she was seen by a doctor and by the police. The woman was Susan Christie. She told the police that she and Penny McAllister had been walking the dogs in the forest. She had paused to tie her shoelace while Penny walked on, following the dogs. When Susan resumed her walk, she said she had come round a corner to see Penny lying on the ground with a man bending over her. Thinking Penny had fallen and that the man was offering help, she came closer. Then she saw blood. At that point, as she stood, 'transfixed', the man turned on her. He grabbed her, pushed her to the ground, and attempted to rape her. He pulled at her tracksuit trousers, and cut open her knickers with his knife, at the same time wounding her in the leg. She screamed for help, shouting 'Daddy! Daddy!' in an effort to make him think her father was close behind. One of the dogs then came back, and while the man was briefly distracted, she kneed him in the testicles; he let go, and ran away.

This story, begun at Ballynahinch, was maintained and elaborated upon by Susan Christie in subsequent interviews with the police, including a visit to the scene of the killing. It was a clearly told account, including a graphic description of the man, whom she described in a way that managed to be quite individual-sounding and yet could apply to a great many young men: average height, slightly built, with short, layered brown hair, blue eyes, stubbled cheeks; and wearing jeans, a Barbour jacket and white trainers. Later she would add that she had seen him again as she fled from the forest, watching her from a hillock. 'I shall never forget these eyes,' she said. Soon afterwards, a witness claimed to have seen such a man driving away from Drumkeeragh Forest in a white Ford Escort XR2 car – an easily identifiable vehicle. But it was never traced.

A massive manhunt was immediately set in motion, but despite the detail of her story, the detectives assigned to the case were unconvinced. The more they probed, the more their suspicions grew. Susan Christie had been wearing leather gloves, but her hands underneath had been blood-stained. She had superficial wounds which, the doctor who examined her confirmed, could have been self-inflicted.

What was beyond all doubt was that Penny McAllister had met a death of extreme violence. Her throat was cut so deeply that her head had almost been severed from her body. The murder weapon, a butcher's boning knife, was found some 800 feet from the body. It was not the kind of knife that would normally be taken on a woodland stroll.

It was not long before the police, probing into the relationship between the two women, found that the background to their apparent friendship was an unusual one. Since the summer of 1990, Captain McAllister and Susan Christie had been lovers. McAllister, a tall, good-looking, athletic officer, and an accomplished sub-aqua diver, had started a diving club at the base in Armagh where he had been stationed since 1989, and Susan Christie had been an early member. Penny McAllister was also an accomplished diver. She was tall, slender and attractive; prettier than but not so gregarious as the smaller, bouncy Susan.

Susan fell for McAllister and made sure he knew of her attraction. The flattered officer and the smitten private soon became lovers. In McAllister's view, the relationship may have been an opportunistic one, but he pursued it vigorously. Once the police had broken Susan's story of the knife-wielding rapist, she gave them a full account of her lovemaking with McAllister – in woods, in cars, even underwater on one occasion when McAllister's wife was present but unaware of what they were doing. This occurred in October during a two-week stay on Ascension Island, where McAllister had taken his diving team on an army- sponsored trip. Penny McAllister was, however, aware that something was going on between her husband and Susan Christie. There was a degree of estrangement, to the extent that earlier that autumn, when she had had a miscarriage in the early stage of pregnancy, she concealed both the pregnancy and the miscarriage from her husband.

Despite her relationship with McAllister, Susan Christie accused another soldier, a senior NCO, of sexual harassment; and on her testimony the man was reprimanded and reduced in rank. Possibly it was her means of deflecting attention from what was really going on between her and McAllister – sexual contact between officers and 'other ranks' at that time was still an offence against military discipline. Following the Ascension Island trip, McAllister, reproached by Penny for his obvious attentions to Susan, told his lover that they needed a cooling-off period. A few days later, she told him she was pregnant. They discussed options. McAllister stated at the trial that he had outlined three possible options to Susan. None of them was what she wanted to hear, namely that he would leave Penny for her. Susan announced that she would have an abortion.

Meanwhile the cooling-off period was forgotten and they resumed an active sex life, taking advantage of all Penny's absences, and crossing to England for a weekend together when he was a delegate at a diving conference in Portsmouth. Then, on 5 December, Susan called McAllister, ostensibly from a hospital, to say she had had a miscarriage. The pregnancy was almost certainly a phantom pregnancy – a gambit to win McAllister's commitment – but it did not work and Susan's tack now changed. It seemed clear that McAllister was not willing to give up Penny for her. To his surprise, she now began to make friendly overtures to Penny. Previously her attitude had been hostile and sarcastic. Susan's effort was strong enough for Penny to confide the story of her miscarriage. But Penny did not tell her new friend that she hadn't told her husband about it. When

Susan angrily accused him of not telling her of his wife's miscarriage, he was astounded to learn of it.

At this stage, McAllister seems to have decided that his adventure with the bouncy little private had gone on for long enough. He encouraged Susan in her ambition to apply for an officer training course. She was accepted for this and was due to commence the course in England in April 1991. McAllister himself was due for promotion. He arranged a skiing holiday for Penny and himself in February 1991. Although he had told Susan that the affair must end, they continued as lovers, though more sporadically than before, while Susan maintained her illusory friendship with Penny. By now, her jealousy of the other woman, better-looking, better-natured, and who still retained the love of her husband, was at white heat. McAllister was alarmed when Susan proposed a diving trip with Penny. He knew well how easy it was to effect an 'accident' in deep water. (Indeed, Susan Christie was to claim in court she had once feared that Penny McAllister was going to kill her during a dive.)

March 1991 was a month of crucial decisions for Susan Christie. On 1 April, her training course was due to begin. She threatened to abandon it, but McAllister was unmoved. What persuaded Penny to go on a walk with her rival in a lonely upland forest is not known, but it is likely that Susan had said there were matters they should discuss in private. Before setting out, she equipped herself with the knife, its five-inch blade sharpened to razor keenness. Her plan was fully prepared, and she did not hesitate to put it into effect.

Susan Christie was something of an actress, or she would not have obtained Penny McAllister's confidence. Her skill was deployed again during her trial, where she managed to portray herself as a woman wronged by a heartless and self-centred lover. The trial judge was Lord Kelly, and the opposing counsel were John Creaney QC, for the prosecution, and Peter Smyth QC, defending.

There were frequent outbursts of tears from the accused woman, and Lord Justice Kelly treated her with notable consideration. Captain McAllister's evidence in court, awkwardly given, that he had loved her only in 'what could be called a friendship way or as a friend', helped her cause, and her counsel, Mr Creaney, naturally pushed his cross-questioning of the Captain as far as he could in this direction. He then turned to his client. She claimed that McAllister had told her he loved her; that he had forced her to have an abortion. When faced with the central question, her admission that she had killed Penny McAllister, Susan Christie claimed she could only remember isolated parts of the whole episode. She did not recall having the knife. She did not recall approaching her victim from behind and savagely cutting her throat. 'When I left that forest,' she said, 'I honestly believed we'd been attacked, and I did not believe it was me.'

The jury brought in a verdict of guilty and made no recommendation for clemency. The judge, however, sentenced the prisoner to five years in prison. Despite the nature and circumstances of the crime, he said he believed it was an irrational action on Christie's part. His view was not endorsed by the prosecuting authorities, who appealed against the lenient sentence. On appeal, the imprisonment was extended by a further four years. Nevertheless, after only four and a half years in prison, Susan Christie was released, to begin a new identity and a new life.

THE RONANSTOWN
BONDAGE KILLER

One day in 1994, an eight-year-old girl walked into a Garda
station in the Dublin suburb of Ronanstown, a working class
area in the north of the city. The story she told resulted in
two missing persons cases being solved, and exposed a
dangerous double killer. The child, who was accompanied
by a neighbour, went to the station to complain about her
father, who was neglecting her. She told the desk sergeant
that he did not feed her properly, and locked her up in the
garden shed for hours at a time. And he had killed her pet
dog and cat – coming home drunk one night, he had bashed
their heads against the kitchen wall.

The Gardai already knew Michael Bambrick, the little
girl's father. They had interviewed him about a thirty-six-
year-old woman named Mary Cummins, who had disappeared after being seen with him in a pub in July 1992.
They asked the little girl if she could remember seeing her.
To their amazement, she was able to give them a detailed
account of meeting the woman with her father. She recalled
playing with the missing woman's daughter, whom she
correctly named Samantha, in the pub where Bambrick and
Mary Cummins were drinking. Later, after two friends of
the missing woman collected the other child, the girl and
her father went to Mary Cummins' flat. There she had been
given something to eat and drink. Bambrick waited while
the woman changed her clothes, and then brought her home

with him. By the next morning, Bambrick's daughter said, she had gone from the house.

Considering that she had only been seven years old, the little girl's recall of events was remarkable. Moreover it directly contradicted the statement made by her father at the time, in which he claimed that he parted from Mary Cummins at a bus stop, shortly after they left the pub together. There were sinister implications in the girl's information. If Michael Bambrick had killed Mary Cummins, it was a sad end to a tragic life. The missing woman had spent her early years in an orphanage, and then been adopted; her adoptive father was a violent drunkard who regularly beat his wife. With such a bad start in life it is not surprising that Mary Cummins developed a severe drink problem when she grew up. She had sold her house some years previously, after the death of her much older boyfriend, and then squandered the proceeds in a few weeks. Shortly afterwards the authorities took her three children into care, because she was incapable of looking after them. At the time of her disappearance, Mary Cummins was unemployed and living on a single mother's allowance.

Bambrick's daughter was asked about her mother, and replied that she 'went away' when she was six. Behind this statement lay another mystery. Patricia McGauley, the common-law wife of Michael Bambrick, had suddenly vanished about a year before Mary Cummins. She was a heavy drinker like her husband, which often led to heated arguments between the couple. She had been trying to control her alcohol consumption, and was growing restless with Bambrick's laziness and his maltreatment of their two small daughters. On Thursday 12 September 1991, neighbours in the row of terraced houses where the couple lived heard shouts, screams and loud noises coming from the house. They did not take much notice because Michael Bambrick and Patricia McGauley regularly fought after their evenings in the local public house, and after a while the racket ceased. Three days later, Bambrick called into Ronanstown Garda Station and reported his partner was missing. He stated that he had last seen her about 9 p.m. on the night of Friday 13 September, when she went out wearing a mohair cardigan and a black skirt. A woman living next door had glimpsed Patricia McGauley walking past her window at about that time.The Gardai interviewed Bambrick on several more occasions, but there was nothing to contradict his story, although one officer noticed a blood-soaked mattress in an upstairs room. Bambrick was asked about this, and replied that his common-law wife had miscarried in the bed. His explanation was accepted at the time, and the investigation into the woman's disappearance eventually petered out. Patricia McGauley's relatives knew she would not have abandoned her children and were sure somebody had murdered her.

Missing persons cases are not uncommon, and many of us know of somebody who suddenly walked away from his or her life for no apparent reason. But two women had disappeared off the face of the earth within ten months, both after last being seen with the same man. The Gardai thought that something far more sinister than a change of air was involved. The McGauley and Cummins' files were reopened and a team of detectives began investigating the man they now suspected of two murders. Michael Bambrick was born in England in 1952, but moved to Dublin when he was five years old. He had been a difficult child and prone to tantrums. Since leaving school, Bambrick had supported himself through unemployment benefits and any casual work he could get. He had got married at the age of twenty, but the relationship failed within a few years. The Gardai interviewed Bambrick's first wife during their inquiries, and discovered some interesting facts about his sexual tastes. She said that two years after they were married, she discovered her husband was a transvestite, when she came home unexpectedly to find him wearing her clothes. Bambrick's tendencies aggravated the problems in a relationship that was already in trouble due to his drinking and inability to find work. He would not agree to go for psychiatric help, and the marriage began to disintegrate. One night, after a particularly ferocious row, she woke up to find herself pinned to the bed by Bambrick, who was wearing her blouse and skirt. He wrapped her tights around her throat and stuffed their ends into her mouth. He let his wife choke until she blacked out, and when she regained consciousness forced her to have sexual intercourse with him. The assault terrified the woman and she left with their child shortly afterwards, fearing that the next time he would kill her. Not long afterwards, in 1975, Bambrick indecently assaulted one of his wife's friends, and was placed on probation.

Between 1975 and the disappearance of Patricia McGauley in 1991, Bambrick had not come to the attention of the police. But in early 1995, Bambrick was arrested for physically abusing his daughter. The Gardai also questioned him about the fates of Patricia McGauley and Mary Cummins whilst he was in custody. Bambrick denied any knowledge of their whereabouts, and gave the Gardai permission to search his house. The house of Frederick West, the notorious English serial killer, had recently given up its gruesome secrets, and the Irish police thought they might find two or more bodies on Bambrick's premises.

The Gardai were eager to begin, but obtaining permission to enter the building from Dublin Corporation took longer than they expected. Bambrick had sublet his corporation house to another couple, and legal regulations dictated that they must be allowed time to move out.

It was April 1995 before the house was finally vacated for the Gardai search team to move in and excavate the small terraced property. The interior was taken apart, and the garden dug up with a JCB digger, but after several days it was apparent that no human remains were hidden there. All that had come to light were the bones of a dog in a shallow grave in the garden, thought to belong to the slaughtered pet of Bambrick's daughter. The search was temporarily abandoned. The failure to uncover any incriminating evidence was something of an embarrassment for the Gardai. The media had been alerted to the inquiry, and the high profile activities in the house in Ronanstown were featured extensively in the press and on television. When nothing was turned up, comparisons were drawn with a suspected triple murder in Cork a few years previously. In that case, one of the missing bodies had been removed from a patch of ground and burnt because the Gardai neglected to guard the area at night.

The officers in charge of the Bambrick investigation were still convinced that he had murdered the two missing women in the Ronanstown house, even if he had disposed of the bodies elsewhere. They changed tack, and brought in forensic experts to give the rooms a thorough scientific examination. There were traces of blood on dozens of floorboards, particularly in the small spare room upstairs. It was in here that an officer had found the bloodstained mattress some years previously.

With this – the first tangible proof that a murder had taken place – the inquiry gathered momentum. The pressure began to worry Bambrick, who had found a new girlfriend and was now living with her. This woman was interviewed and stated that her boyfriend's sexual tastes leaned towards bondage. Moreover, Bambrick had told her he killed a woman one night, although he would not reveal the details of what had happened. When the Gardai delved into the suspect's recent activities, they received a very disturbing complaint. He was accused of indecently assaulting a fifteen-year-old girl in 1994, and there were unsubstantiated reports of interference with much younger children. Detectives also discovered he was in possession of an illegally held shotgun, a very serious crime in Ireland which usually results in a custodial sentence. Bambrick was placed under twenty-four-hour surveillance, and in the last week of June he was arrested on firearms charges under the Offences Against the State Act.

Once he was in custody, the team of detectives investigating the two missing women gave him a full interrogation. They confronted the suspect with the circumstantial evidence against him, backed up by the information they had gathered about his sexual habits. Bambrick denied everything at first, but suddenly cracked and admitted he had killed the two women in bondage sessions. He described how he had tied Patricia McGauley's hands together with her tights, and then stuffed the legs down her throat. According to Bambrick's account, her death had been an accident; the victim began to choke and died before he could remove the tights. He hid the body of his common-law wife in the spare bedroom, and left it there for the next two days. On the evening after the death, he dressed up in her clothes and a wig, and then went out of the house. He knew his neighbours would assume they had seen Patricia McGauley, and support his story to the police. On the following day, he disposed of the corpse, which he cut up into pieces with a hacksaw and stuffed into two plastic bags. Bambrick wheeled the first bag on his bicycle to the Dublin Corporation Dump at Balgaddy, and then returned home for the second bag. He hid some of the remains under piles of rubbish and buried the rest. On his second trip to the dump, the killer noticed the victim's head was exposed; he smashed it with a concrete block and buried the fragments. The death of Mary Cummins followed much the same pattern, although this time Bambrick buried the remains in a field about half a mile away from the dump.

That evening, Michael Bambrick showed detectives the places where he had concealed the bodies of his two victims. The Balgaddy Dump had been cleared in the years since the death of Pauline McGauley, but after an extensive search the Gardai uncovered one of her teeth, a rib and fragments of skull. They discovered more extensive remains of Mary Cummins, including her severed thighbones. They were still wrapped in the remains of a coloured suspender belt and black nylons. There was no evidence to show how either woman had died, and Bambrick continued to insist that he had not intended killing them. As a consequence, it was felt safer to try him for manslaughter rather than murder.

In July 1996, he was sentenced to eighteen years' imprisonment, the maximum term the judge could give him.

THE BLACK WIDOW FACTOR

'Hit-men' have long been familiar from movies and novels, but until the rise of organized crime in recent years they were almost unknown in Ireland. But, since 1980, the hired assassin has become more common on these shores, adding to the burden on Garda resources since such killers are difficult to track down. Most 'hits' take place in the shadowy world of drug dealers, and arise from feuds between the various 'gang lords' who control the illegal trade. But there have also been several domestic murders where men have been paid to kill an unwanted husband or wife. One such case, involving the death of a Wicklow publican, led to the first great murder trial of the new millennium.

'Jack White's', a few miles north of the town of Arklow, is one of the best-known public houses in County Wicklow. Around 4.30 a.m. on 19 March 1996, two days after St Patrick's Day, a Garda patrol car, responding to an alarm call, arrived on the premises to find its owner, Tom Nevin, lying dead on the floor of a back room. His wife Catherine was found tied up in her bedroom. Pieces of her valuable collection of jewellery were scattered around the room, and her television set was dumped on an upstairs landing. Tom Nevin had been counting the day's takings, and a sum of £30,000 was missing. So was his car, which had been stolen from the car park beside the premises. The publican had been killed by a shotgun blast to the heart at point blank range; nine pellets were removed from his chest and he was estimated to have died within four minutes. Catherine Nevin told the Gardai that an armed man had roughly woken her earlier in the night, and demanded to know where she kept her valuables. A second burglar came into the room, and she was tied up and gagged. The men left, and a little while later she heard a bang, followed by the sounds of two cars starting up and leaving. She tried to untie her bonds but they were too tight, and it had taken her a while to crawl to a panic button and activate it.

From this account, it seemed that the Nevins had been the victims of an armed robbery. Public houses were attractive targets for thieves, and Dublin gangs had robbed a number of rural establishments in recent years. They would expect to find large sums of cash on premises like Jack White's, especially on a busy Bank Holiday weekend. The theory that Dublin burglars had murdered Tom Nevin received further credence when his abandoned car was found in the city. On the other hand, there were several anomalies in the crime that worried the police. The first was the ease with which the robbers entered the public house. A second was why none of Catherine Nevin's jewellery had been taken. The thieves had apparently left the whole collection behind them. The Gardai began to wonder if there might be more to the murder than met the eye.

Tom Nevin, the evidence suggested, had been deliberately gunned down in cold blood. There was no sign that the victim had put up any resistance, and he appeared to have been taken completely by surprise. The murder resembled a professional gangland 'hit', and the police began to wonder if the real motive of the intruder was to kill Tom Nevin rather than rob him. Their attention was soon directed towards

Catherine Nevin, who was rumoured to be unhappy with her husband. A number of minor discrepancies in her story spurred this interest, as did a name one of the detectives noticed in an open notebook belonging to the widow. It belonged to a known IRA activist with alleged criminal connections in the Dublin underworld. The Gardai began gathering evidence against the woman they now suspected may have been implicated in the murder of her husband.

Catherine Nevin was in her mid-forties in 1996, and had been married to Tom Nevin for nearly twenty years. She came from a comparatively humble Kildare farming background, but had transformed herself into a sophisticated, well-groomed and exceptionally competent businesswoman. Alongside her husband, a Galway man, she had expanded Jack White's with a restaurant and facilities for guests. Catherine Nevin was largely responsible for the success of these new ventures. Over the years, she had forged good relationships with the local community, and was liked and respected by most of her customers. There was, however, a darker side to her personality. Like many self-made people she was a social climber and something of a snob. Her obsession with her personal appearance irritated some of her acquaintances, as did the flaunting of her wealth and possessions. There was also some gossip about her love life, and she was rumoured to be sleeping with several local dignitaries.

Anybody who got to know her well soon learnt she despised her husband, and often complained about his drinking and failure to do his share of running the pub. The deterioration in the relationship between the couple seems to have dated back to a few years after their wedding. It is hard to fathom why she so loathed Tom Nevin, a quiet, hard-working man whose main interest in life outside of the pub was Gaelic sports. But by 1990 Catherine Nevin had embarked on a series of affairs, and was plotting to have her husband murdered. At that time, the Nevins were running a public house in the working-class Dublin suburb of Finglas, and they had made the acquaintance of a number of known criminals and IRA members. It became apparent to the Gardai, as they investigated further, that Catherine Nevin had the underworld contacts to hire a killer. She also had a strong motive – if her husband died she would inherit his property and have sole ownership of the pub. They had failed to track down the person who put the gun to Tom Nevin's heart, yet they had gathered enough evidence to implicate his wife as the guiding force behind the crime. Catherine Nevin was arrested and charged with the murder of Tom Nevin, and on three counts of soliciting his murder.

The first attempt to try her for the crime – in January 2000 – was abandoned after a few days, when it was discovered that conversations between jurors had been overheard in the Public Gallery of the courtroom. Intense media attention had been focused on Catherine Nevin, and her clothes and demeanour attracted much adverse publicity. This was felt to be detrimental to the accused receiving a fair hearing. Unusually strong restrictions were placed on the press reporting of the second trial, which took place in March and April 2000. Few Irish court cases have been as sensational, or taken such unexpected twists and turns. During its course, a district court judge and a retired senior policeman took the stand to deny they had been Catherine Nevin's lovers, whilst no less than three men testified that she had solicited them to kill Tom Nevin between 1989 and 1991. The State prosecutor pointed out inconsistencies found at the murder scene, and questioned the long delay between the shooting and Catherine Nevin alerting the Gardai. Mrs Nevin had failed to bring the previous day's takings to the bank, so there was more money than normal on the premises. Staff members testified to her bad relationship with her husband, and said she had warned them not to return after sending them off to a disco that night. A carpet layer, who was working in Jack White's, remembered Catherine Nevin's constant complaints about her husband; on numerous occasions she had said she wanted him dead.

It is unlikely that this circumstantial evidence would have been enough to convict Catherine Nevin on its own. The keystone of the Prosecution's case was the testimony of the three men whom it was claimed she had previously asked to kill her husband.

As well as providing the basis of three further charges against her, their accounts showed she had been actively planning the murder of her husband. None of these witnesses might have seemed particularly credible at first, since they all had previous criminal convictions or connections to Sinn Fein and the IRA. Neither were their memories always reliable; one of them was unable to remember in what year the approaches took place, and had to ask the judge if she would 'settle for the century?' Yet each was very clear in testifying that Catherine Nevin had offered him a large sum of money to kill Tom Nevin on more than one occasion. And their accounts contained a number of personal details about the couple, which could only have come directly from the woman in the dock.

Perhaps the strongest witness for the prosecution was Catherine Nevin herself. Designer suits, perfect make-up and coiffured hair seemed inappropriate in the circumstances.

She was not, after all, a film star appearing before her public; Catherine Nevin was on trial for the premeditated and callous murder of another human being. Her self-composure and indifference to the devastating evidence against her were also remarkable. This encouraged what her counsel called the 'Black Widow' factor – a negative attitude to the accused based on her demeanour in court.

Catherine Nevin's testimony in the witness box was disastrous for the defence. Although claiming she had loved her husband, she blackened his memory by conjuring up a hitherto unmentioned criminal link with the IRA. Her statement that Tom Nevin laundered money for the organization was seen for what it was – a shoddy attempt to shift the blame for his murder away from herself. The alleged IRA connection was also brought forward to explain the single most bizarre incident of this extraordinary trial. On 16 March, Catherine Nevin, who was about to enter her third day in the witness box, did not appear in court. It transpired that she had been taken sick on the previous evening at her home, and rushed to a hospital. The patient was found to have overdosed on a cocktail of prescription drugs, mixed (or so the prosecution claimed) with washing-up liquid.

When Mrs Nevin resumed giving her evidence a week later, the judge sent the jury away and demanded an explanation. The accused told him that on the night of 15 March she had arrived home to find a strange man in the house. She recognized him as a friend of her husband but did not know his name. After warning her that she 'was naming people she shouldn't be naming in court, that she was causing problems for people, and she wasn't going to name any more people', the intruder took a handful of tablets from his pocket and proceeded to force them down her throat. Her rambling explanation was so ludicrous and patently untrue that her credibility was destroyed. With it she removed any doubts that the journalists and spectators in the public gallery might have had about who killed her husband.

The jury in the case took over four days to reach a verdict – the longest deliberation ever recorded in an Irish court. Many observers expected them to return and tell the judge that they could not agree on a verdict. In fact, they unanimously found Catherine Nevin guilty of murder and one soliciting charge, and returned 11:1 majority verdicts of guilty on the other two soliciting charges. Justice Carroll sentenced her to life imprisonment. To date, the person who pulled the trigger on that night in 1996 has not been arrested. It also seems certain that the killer had at least one accomplice, since a second man would be required to drive the publican's car. The Gardai believe that an associate of one of the big Dublin crime gangs killed Tom Nevin. One likely suspect is a well-known hit man who is at present serving a long sentence for his part in another murder. But unless Catherine Nevin confesses, and names the man she paid to kill her husband, there is little chance he will ever be brought to book.